THE **GOOD** DIVORCE

*How to consciously create
the best possible outcome
for you and your family*

BY
ANDREW SILVERT &
BECKY SHOOK-WOTZKA

CONTRIBUTIONS BY SONIKA TINKER

To the twists &
turns of life!
— Becky Shook-Wotzka

Blessings or your love journey!

Dear Karen,

Thank you so much for your
friendship, love, and support. I
wish for you your heart's desire.
I Love You. Andy 2/22/14

DEDICATIONS

Andy's Dedication

To my parents, Paula & Steve, who unwittingly modeled a Good Divorce to their kids at a time when divorce was still a taboo subject;

To my sons, David and Zachary, for inspiring Keiko and I to be our best selves throughout our divorce process;

To Keiko, who has been my willing and supportive partner in co-creating our Good Divorce;

To Brian and Rachael Jeffries for their unconditional support and friendship during and since our divorce, and for the heartfelt Foreword to this book;

To Holly Holt for her detailed and insightful editing skills;

To Becky, for her experience, expertise, and dedication to creating this book;

To Sonika, whose workshop inspired the idea for this book and whose brilliant contribution provided the missing piece to the Good Divorce puzzle.

Becky's Dedication

To my mom, Debbie Hannan, whose idea it was to start our business. Without that idea this book would have never been;

To my husband, Jeffrey Wotzka, who has never wavered in supporting my decision to be who I am and do what I do;

To Ryan Frost, for taking time to help edit this book, and for making our business the success it has become;

To Andy, for his attention to detail, creative ideas, and on-going demand for excellence that will allow readers everywhere to have a Good Divorce;

To Lee Scott, for connecting Andy and I. Also for his generous monetary donation to this project;

To my other work partners, Nicolina Cahouette, Dawn Solem-Hanley, Staci Bartley-Welch, Nicole Welch, and Wade Hanley for contributing to our business and shaping the ideas in this book;

And to my clients, who have been my inspiration in making an on-going difference, and in teaching the lessons that are so easily shared in this book now!

———∞———

Cover concept by Andrew Silvert
Cover illustration by Tania Von Allmen

CONTENTS

Dedications · iii

Foreword · vii

Why we Wrote this Book · · · · · · · · · · · · · · · · · · · xi

How to Read this Book · xv

1 Secrets to a Good Divorce · · · · · · · · · · · · · · · · · · ·1

2 Divorce Myths ·7

3 A Good Divorce *(Andrew's Story)* · · · · · · · · · · · · · · 15

4 Today's Typical Divorce: A Tragic Tale *(Becky's Story)* · · · · ·23

5 The System - Playing The Game · · · · · · · · · · · · · ·29

6 Mediators & Lawyers · 39

7 The Uncooperative Spouse · · · · · · · · · · · · · · · · · 49

8 Financials: Assets, Liabilities, & Support · · · · · · · · · · · 69

9 The Kids ·81

10 Choosing Your Team ·91

11 The Divorce Process Revealed · · · · · · · · · · · · · · · 103

12 Managing The Emotional Transition · · · · · · · · · · · · 109

Appendix I Assessing Whether You Are In
Marriage Breakdown · 117

Appendix II Your Good Divorce Check List · · · · · · · · 125

About the Authors · 127

FOREWORD

I have known Andy and Keiko for almost 20 years. They are the reason my wife and I met in 1994. So when Andy told me that his marriage was coming to an end after 16 years, I was shocked. In many ways, Andy and Keiko seemed like the model couple. They were always loving and supportive of each other. They never seemed to get into petty arguments. They never ever spoke to, or of, each other in a way that was disrespectful or contemptuous.

The two of them, splitting up, did not make any sense.

But I also knew that Andy was unhappy. I didn't know why and I am not sure that he did either. He did explain that he and Keiko seemed to want different things and that they could not figure out how to be happy staying together. It seemed a little silly to me and I assumed that they would figure it all out and eventually reconcile.

My wife and I visited Andy, Keiko, and their boys several times while they were breaking up. There was sometimes tension, but never any of the yelling and screaming that I had come to expect from media images of divorcing couples. As the reality of their breakup seemed to settle in, the tension lifted and they seemed to become even better friends than they had been before. They even covered each other's childcare duties so that the other partner could go on dates!

Through it all, their sons seemed to go on as if everything were "normal." I am sure that they had some difficulties, but they never seemed to be victims of a broken family, just kids learning how to manage the complicated logistics of their new living arrangements.

This mystified me. I knew that there was no way that I could do the same if my marriage ever came to an end.

Fast forward a few years, and I was feeling very unhappy and unfulfilled in my marriage. I began to feel that if I wanted to be happy, I had no choice but to divorce my wife. But since I had Andy and Keiko's example of how to be divorced, I knew that I did not have to explode my family in order to end my marriage. I knew that my wife and I could take care of the children, together, while making space for our needs as individual adults. I knew that we could take actions that might be inconvenient but which would care for the other partner's needs. I understood that even though we would be divorcing, we would forever be a family because we would always be joined by children and probably grandchildren. And if we wanted to be happy people, we needed to ensure that our family unit, while differently configured than we had hoped and planned, would continue to be healthy. Whatever that meant.

So with Andy and Keiko as our model, my wife and I planned our separation together. We worked together to create new living arrangements for ourselves (the children stayed in the house, the adults rotated in on a weekly basis), we made the children's interests primary, and we took care to communicate with each other. We got some professional counseling to help us split up.

When we actually physically separated, we continued to communicate well. Like Andy and Keiko, we took care to be respectful of spoken and unspoken boundaries. We treated each other as we wished to be treated.

After about 6 months of physical separation, we decided that we really do work well together. So we reconciled. It was not very dramatic; we just let go of the separate apartment and went back to sleeping in the same house. It just felt like the right thing to do.

That reconciliation was only possible because we took care to not harm each other while we were breaking up. Of course we hurt each other a bit... that is to be expected. But since we went out of our way to avoid being malicious, it was easy to offer and accept apologies for those hurt feelings.

Andy and Keiko did not get my wife and I back together. But their example kept us from burning the bridge that was our love and friendship. We chose to walk back across that bridge to be together, and that is why I say that their divorce saved our marriage.

- Brian Jeffries

WHY WE WROTE THIS BOOK

Andy's "Why"

My ex-wife and I are friends. Our kids are whole. Our divorce cost us about $400[1]. We still share the same mutual friends. My parents still treat Keiko as their daughter. Based on what I see out in the world, we are unusual. We are the exception. For many people, divorce is messy, damaging, and hurtful. But does it really have to be that way? Both of us have many friends, colleagues and acquaintances who are going through the divorce process. My ex-wife and I are often asked, "How did you do it? How did you guys have such a 'good' divorce? What was your secret?" My purpose in co-writing this book is to answer these questions.

Becky's "Why"

Unlike Andy, I grew up around some very painful divorces. The kind of divorces where kids are evicted from their homes two days before Christmas because some judge decided he wanted to give the house to the "other spouse." The kind of divorces where

---

[1] Cost of the mediator and court filing in Sacramento, CA 2006

ex-spouses stopped talking to one another despite 20 years of history and kids in the picture. The kind of divorces where a child can go years without talking to one parent because of the guilt of betraying the other parent.

I did not believe there could be a better "model" for divorce. Yet, I had hope. And one day that hope resulted in my becoming a divorce mediator. People now ask me all of the time: "Is it really possible to have a 'friendly' divorce?" Just as Andy acknowledged, many people are surprised to discover that there is such a thing as a "good" divorce.

So we wanted to write this book to reveal the secrets of the Good Divorce as a real possibility – an alternative to fighting, bickering over who gets the end-table, and abusing our kids over who loves them more.

Your "Why"

If you have picked up this book, you are most likely contemplating a divorce, in the midst of a divorce, or reeling from the negative impacts of the traditional family law system. We are here for you. We know the depths of negative emotions that have and may continue to surface. If you have children, we understand that you worry about what your divorce will do or has done to them. We also know that you are either fearful of losing a significant portion of your income or of losing the money that you had access to within your family system.

You could be in a space of giving up and walking away from everything, or you may want to fight for what is "rightly" yours. You could even want revenge against the very person you loved at one time. Lastly, you could be considering divorce, but the uncertain future has you paralyzed in fear.

There is no ONE answer on what is the right path to a Good Divorce. This book is written to explore many answers to the question: "What is the secret to a Good Divorce?" It discusses many choices, options for how you might approach this time of transition in your life, and decisions that might lead to a better ending. It will give you ideas that can be translated into action today.

We ask that, as you read, you keep an open mind. With an open mind, you will be able to find the most creative approach for you. Do not rule out an option just because you think your spouse will not do it. Do not reject an idea because it seems like too much work. The only way to a new life is through the pain of the transition. You can choose to deal with it now; you can choose to deal with it in your next relationship; or you can choose to carry on in debilitating numbness and let it hold you back from having another relationship in the future.

Are you ready to walk with us through this journey toward a healthier, transformational, and dare we say Good Divorce? Ask yourself these questions: "What if this journey could transform the lives of my family for the better? What if this journey could create a next generation of children who have learned to exit relationships as amicably as they entered them? What if this journey could make the world a little bit better by reducing the amount of pain and suffering in the world?

We welcome you to explore this new possibility as we walk you through the steps to create a Good Divorce.

HOW TO READ THIS BOOK

The chapters in this book have been strategically placed in order to help you through your divorce process from beginning to end. Depending on where you are in this process, you may want to read every chapter, skip a chapter, or go directly to a specific chapter.

Chapter 1 starts right off with one of the most important secrets in creating a Good Divorce. This chapter discusses Stephen Covey's technique of beginning with the end in mind as applied to divorce. You will be encouraged to think through your end in mind, explore your areas of influence, and minimize worrying about things that are outside of your control. We suggest what a Good Divorce might look like from our perspective and ask the question "what would a Good Divorce look like for you and your spouse?"

In Chapter 2, we talk about the most common myths that people have about divorce in this country. This chapter will help you to perceive the process of divorce with an open mind where all possibilities are considered.

In Chapter 3, you will have the opportunity to hear Andy's story, and see a Good Divorce in action. The positive impact on

Andy's kids are apparent through his own son's testimonial of how Andy and Keiko handled their divorce.

Chapter 4, in stark contrast to Andy's story, presents a fictional, but representative story about the tragedy of how divorces often play out today. This book teaches you how to avoid this unfortunate path.

In Chapter 5, you will learn about the endless maze of the court system. Mentally put yourself through this experience and ask yourself if it is really what you want for yourself, your kids, your extended family members, and even your ex.

In Chapter 6, you will learn about the difference between mediators and lawyers. Learn how mediation works and where it may be appropriate to utilize lawyers.

Chapter 7 will help you deal with an uncooperative spouse, or situations where you believe your spouse will not cooperate. This chapter can be your saving grace in helping you and your partner work together as a team to create a Good Divorce.

Chapter 8 is chock full of all the things you need to know about your finances during divorce. This information is based on personal experiences with clients (it is NOT legal advice). This chapter also explains the "secret" process of dividing your assets and liabilities fairly, without fighting.

If you have kids, **Chapter 9** is the most important chapter you can read, read again, and read yet again. How you handle your divorce process and subsequent co-parenting with your ex will have a significant impact on the quality of life of your children. Learn how to take the high road and behave in a way that protects your children from harm's way.

Chapter 10 will teach you how to select your divorce team. This is one of the most critical times in your life and who you choose to surround yourself with will make all the difference in how easily you move through the divorce process and your own transition to a brighter future.

Chapter 11 lays out the entire divorce process and helps you figure out the best way to navigate the various pathways through this process. It is numbered and lettered to correspond to a visual chart that you can download from our website.

In Chapter 12, you will learn about the natural process of grief in divorce, and techniques for moving yourself along the transition curve. Take care of yourself. As they say on the airplane, "be sure to put your oxygen mask on first." Otherwise, how can you be of any help to others?

Let's get started! Here's to creating your Good Divorce!

Note on Pronoun Conventions Used in this Book

This book is a collaborative effort. We have used the following "voice" conventions to help clarify who is talking when pronouns are used. In Chapter 3, "I" and "my" always refer to Andy. In Chapter 4, "I" and "my" always refer to Becky. In Chapter 7, "I" and "my" always refer to Sonika. In all other chapters in the book, when "I" or "my" is first used in a paragraph or a section, the speaker is identified in parenthesis. The use of "we" or "our" throughout the book refers to all of us together.

Chapter 1

SECRETS TO A GOOD DIVORCE

S o, you are getting divorced. Welcome to this not-so-exclusive
club.

Have you thought about what kind of a divorce you actually
want to have? Do you want a divorce that is painful, expensive, and
damaging to your children – one that makes you and your former
spouse miserable for years to come? A divorce like so many others in our society today where a worst-case outcome seems to have
become the dreaded, expected, and accepted norm?

Or would you like to have a divorce that is relatively painless
and drama free, not more expensive than it needs to be, and one
that leaves your children and your mutual friendships whole? One
in which you can actually be friends or at least amicable with your
former spouse? One in which you can be effective co-parents for
your children? The kind of divorce that seems to be "the impossible
dream?"

So, we ask you again, what kind of a divorce do you actually want to have? Just asking this question creates the possibility that you have a choice in the matter! You are actually empowered to choose and to ultimately create your divorce experience to be as positive as possible. The purpose of this book is to show you how to do this!

The famous self-help guru and author, Steven Covey, in his book *The Seven Habits of Highly Successful People*, talks about the habit of "starting with the end in mind." Why is this important and what does this mean in the context of divorce? Well, if you do not have a vision of what you want, of where you want to go, then how do you expect to get there? If you do not set an intention and commit to having a Good Divorce, then you can't realistically expect to have one. But how many people actually do this?

To begin with the end in mind with anything, including a divorce, means to start with a clear picture and understanding of your desired final destination. It means to know where you are going (follow your map) so that you better understand where you are now. This means the steps you take and the decisions that you make along the way are always in support of your desired outcome. Imagine how different things could be in our lives if we really focused on what was most important to us and managed ourselves each day to be and do what really matters most.

Covey says, "Beginning with the end in mind is based on the principle that all things are created twice. There is a mental, or first creation, and a physical, or second creation, to all things." It's a principle that states all things are created twice, but not all first creations are by conscious design. In our personal lives, especially around emotionally stressful situations such as divorce, if we do not develop our own self-awareness and become responsible for our first creations, we empower other people (spouse, lawyers, courts, etc.) and circumstances outside of our control to impact and shape our lives by default. Whether we are aware of it or not, whether we are in control of it or not, there is a first creation to every part of our lives. As Covey writes, "We are either the second creation of our own proactive first creation, or we are the second creation of other people's agendas, of circumstances, or of past beliefs and habits."

Whether it is building a house, starting a business, raising our kids, or getting divorced, understanding and following this principle is critical to getting what we want in life.

Do you want a Good Divorce? Then you have to commit to creating one! Do you want a Good Divorce? Then you have to plan on having one. Do you want a Good Divorce? Then you have to follow your Good Divorce plan!

Covey also defines something called the "Circle of Concern/ Influence." This concept is critical to understand if you want to create a Good Divorce with your soon-to-be ex-spouse.

We all have a wide range of concerns – our health, our children, our job, our marriage, the state of the economy and the environment. We could separate these from things in which we have no particular mental or emotional connection by creating a "Circle of Concern." Looking at things in our Circle of Concern, it is clear that there are some things over which we have no real control and others that we might be able to do something about. We could identify those things that we have some influence over by putting them within a smaller circumscribed "Circle of Influence." Effective people (those who positively create what they want in their lives) focus their efforts on their Circle of Influence. They work on things that they can do something about. The nature of their energy is positive, enlarging, magnifying and this causes their Circle of Influence to increase.

Reactive people on the other hand (most people going through a divorce behave re-actively) often focus their efforts outside of the Circle of Influence. They focus on the faults of their spouse, the past problems in their relationship and on circumstances over which they have no control. As Covey says, "This focus results in blaming and accusations, reactive language, and increased feelings of victimization. The negative energy created by this focus, combined with neglect in areas they could actually do something about, causes their circle of influence to shrink."

So to create a Good Divorce:

1. Make an intention to have a Good Divorce – start with the end in mind

2. Always work from your Circle of Influence

3. Have a clear picture (definition) of what a Good Divorce looks like for you and your soon-to-be former spouse

What does a good divorce look like for you? For us (Andy and Keiko), our Good Divorce looked like this:

• Our kids were undamaged by the process – even enriched by the experience.

- We spent very little money on the entire process – about $400[2].

- We did not use lawyers or go to court.

- We were both satisfied with the terms of our divorce and have both honored those terms since the divorce.

- We have both maintained all of our mutual friends.

- We are still friends, in fact maybe even better friends, than when we were married.

What does your Good Divorce look like? Only you know the answer to that question! Imagine it, visualize it, feel it, write it down and share it with your spouse. That is the first step to making it into your reality.

Please visit the Good Divorce website (www.thegooddivorcebook. com) to download our handy "Design your own Good Divorce" worksheet.

---

[2] Cost of the mediator and legal separation court filing in Sacramento, CA 2006

Chapter 2

DIVORCE MYTHS

O ur experience is that our beliefs are often invisible to us, that
we take many of them for granted as facts without investi-
gating whether they are "true" or not.

The Wikipedia dictionary defines "belief" as follows: a mental
acceptance of a claim as truth regardless of supporting evidence.
In his groundbreaking book, *The Biology of Belief,* Dr. Bruce Lipton
presents extensive evidence that our beliefs can and do affect the
structural composition of our cells. The point of this is that our
beliefs, especially our unexamined ones, can have an affect on our
experience of reality. In fact, in many cases our beliefs actually create our reality.

The Wikipedia dictionary defines "myth" as follows: an
unproved or false collective belief. It is not surprising that there are
a number of myths about divorce that many of us just believe to be
true without examination. Since our beliefs can and do create our
reality, it is important to examine our divorce beliefs and prevailing
myths about divorce.

For example, if you believe that you need to hire a lawyer to "protect" your interests in a divorce and do not examine the "truth" of this myth, you are likely to go ahead and hire a lawyer. Andy and his ex did not subscribe to this myth, so they chose not to hire a lawyer and were able to complete their divorce for about $400!

——— ⚭ ———

So what are those common myths about divorce that are not consistent with reality? Let's explore.

Myth #1: You need a lawyer to get divorced. You have to go to court to get a divorce.

Since divorce is primarily treated as an adversarial process in our society, most divorcing couples turn to lawyers as a matter of course. Because of this, the alternatives are unfortunately a hidden secret to many. In this book we examine many alternatives that exist. You do not need a lawyer to get divorced. You may want one, but it is not required. In most cases, we recommend that lawyers be used as a secondary resource to get advice about your legal rights. Their time is NOT best used in settling who gets the dog, how you should co-parent, or by analyzing mountains of financial data to achieve "fairness." We recommend that you use lawyers strategically, not tactically.

Many divorcing people believe they have to go to court at some point in the course of the process. This is not true in many states. Almost all of my (Becky) mediated clients never step into a courtroom. Once in awhile, a judge may ask for a hearing if something in the final papers is unusual, but this is not common.

Myth #2: I don't trust my spouse, so I know we can't work through a divorce in a civil fashion.

Undoubtedly, trust is one of the first things to disappear when a couple decides on a divorce. There is no denying this can be one of the most difficult obstacles to creating a Good Divorce.

We have all heard it said in one way or another that "it is not what happens to you that determines your experience, but rather how you react to what happens to you." You can behave any way you choose. If you do not have trust, you may have to work a little harder to sift through facts and fiction.

The belief that makes this myth seem so real is the idea that if I cannot trust you on one thing, I cannot trust you on anything. Not necessarily.

We find that few people lie about everything. People usually twist the truth thematically. That means there are certain types of things they lie about, or they cover up a truth in reaction to certain emotions. Once you find the theme, you can generally sift through the fiction to find the facts.

In Chapter 7, "The Uncooperative Spouse," we give detailed techniques on how to work through a divorce with your spouse. If trust is an issue, you can use the techniques we have provided to strengthen your trust in your partner again.

Myth #3: Getting divorced will damage your children.

It is not actually divorce that damages kids; it is how the parents handle the divorce process that determines the impact on their children.

Would most people say that it is harder to live in a single household? Probably. However, once in a divorced situation, there are many creative ways to ensure that children are supported in an ongoing way by the family system. For example, many people move back in with parents temporarily or with friends in order to ensure the kids have a community around them.

Is it harder for kids to transfer back and forth between two houses with different rules/structures? Most likely. However, you might look at the situation a little differently. I (Becky) have seen kids gain amazing adaptive skills in learning how to handle different rules within their two homes. Kids who struggle often learn to overcome obstacles, while more sheltered kids often do not. In my interviews with kids about moving between their two parents' houses, many of them respond positively to having two homes; many even view it as a benefit.

Have you heard that kids of divorce end up with less quality parenting time? I know that as a parent, I try even harder now than I ever did before to instill learning skills in my kids because I have to leverage the more limited time I have with them. Did they get a bedtime story when we lived together as a whole family? Not always. Do they get a bedtime story every night they are with me now? You bet.

As Andy's son writes about in the next chapter, it is even possible for kids to be enriched by their divorce experience.

Myth #4: I'm not lovable because my spouse left me, or I will not be able to love again.

If you are divorcing or divorced, there are probably many reasons that contributed to your marriage breakdown.

Some say we select mates to help us heal baggage that we picked up in our childhood. If true, then the very person we are often attracted to is also the very person with whom we are most likely to recreate the same unhealthy patterns from our past.

If you don't do the work to heal, you are likely to run into the same issues again and again in future relationships. In this book, we discuss the importance of taking time to heal, so that we do not repeat the same dysfunctional relationship patterns as before (if you have kids, taking this time will help ensure that they do not unconsciously follow the same patterns in their own life).

The path to loving again is different for everyone. Whether you are the one choosing the divorce or not, you have to heal, take care of yourself and make sure to consciously choose your next relationship. It may be cliché, but we believe you have to learn to love yourself again first, before you can love another. Take care of yourself, and the rest will follow. Some paths to love take longer, because people decide to skip the healing part.

Loving again involves being clear about what you want. Have you taken the time to state your intentions for your next relationship? Have you envisioned what you want? Are you doing the work to attract the relationship that will work for you?

Once you attract the relationship you want (rather than the one that your subconscious wants), the real work begins. Be ready to continue your own self-growth and work through success and pain with your new partner.

Myth #5: I will be financially devastated if I divorce.

You do not have to hire lawyers and battle through divorce. There are more cost-effective ways to divorce than going through an adversarial battle. As you know, all battles have high costs. You just need to choose wisely how you divorce. You were an effective partnership once. You can partner through this phase of your life and successfully deconstruct your marriage as if it were a business.

Can you keep the same lifestyle? Probably not. Will you be financially devastated? No. But you may have to adjust your budget and the types of things you purchase. It can be a humbling experience to go back to your roots and learn to live more minimally. Once you adjust your budget down, you will find yourself able to add savings back in over time. You just have to think and work differently. Eventually, you will find a way to add things back into your life that you had to take out of your budget.

Use the Good Divorce process to keep yourself as financially intact as possible. Mediators are cheaper than lawyers (often much more so), in part because you are paying for one person's time instead of two. And the Good Divorce process includes budgeting, which should assist you to more easily shift your money management style to align with your new divorced life.

While it may not be easy to think differently about money, you can do it. As we discussed in Chapter 1, this is one place where you have great influence in the divorce process. Be smart about the decisions you make before, during, and after the divorce, and you will find that you are less a victim of your circumstances, and more a powerful creator of your desires.

Myths Redefined

If, as we suggest, you create your own reality, then all myths can be dispelled and you have the power to make your divorce a positive experience for all concerned.

If you have already determined divorce is for you, you have an opportunity to end your marriage differently. You can make the choice to end your marriage with grace and dignity, leading to a more powerful life on the other side.

Chapter 3

A GOOD DIVORCE
(*Andrew's Story*[3])

"Your Dad and I are getting a divorce," sobbed my mother as I sat next to her in the car in our driveway. I was 15 and had absolutely no clue this was coming. My parents never fought in front of us. It turned out they were having serious marital issues for several years but had been advised by their shrink to hide their problems from their children "to protect us." The thing was that although we had no conscious awareness of our parent's marital problems, we still felt those problems energetically and emotionally; because we had no idea what the source of our discomfort and stress was, we just internalized it all. We didn't know what questions to ask or whom to ask them to. For years, I beat myself up for not being able to see what was really going on.

---

[3] In some instances, my (Andy) memories and interpretation of these events may not be the same as Keiko's.

When I was old enough to think about such things, I promised myself that I would never get divorced. Yet to my utter dismay, 25 years later, I found myself following in my parent's footsteps. Although I was not able to keep my promise, at least I could go about my divorce process in a completely different way than many of my friends, relatives, and colleagues who were going through their own messy, painful, and expensive divorces.

———— ✆ ————

My former wife, Keiko, and I met on a bus in Kyoto, Japan in 1988. Meeting my future wife on a bus in a foreign country was not something I had ever imagined. Less than two years later, we were married and living together in Tokyo. Our first son, David, was born in 1993. Three years later, we moved to California where I went to graduate school at UC Berkeley. It was here that the cracks in our relationship started to emerge. For the first several years of our marriage, the cultural differences between us were a source of mystery, excitement and attraction for me. At some point, however, the lack of a common cultural background and mutual interests started to take an invisible toll on our relationship. The core problem, for me, however, was our lack of "romantic" chemistry.

Yet despite our "marital" issues, we got along well as friends, did not fight, and in general had a comfortable life that we did not want to lose. Instead of facing our communication and intimacy problems directly, we decided to have another child. I naively thought that this would make things better. Although having another child did mask our issues for a while, things between us continued to deteriorate.

One of the consequences of not dealing with emotional pain and repressed feelings is that these feelings tend to manifest at some point as physical symptoms. In my case, it showed up with the sudden onset (with no apparent physical cause) of excruciating lower back pain and sciatica. I basically became an invalid and Keiko had to take care of me (and our two boys) for over a year while she continued to run her full-time business to support us.

In my darkest moments, I promised God that if I ever recovered, I would be happy, loving, grateful, and a better husband, father, friend, and son. Well, that is not exactly the way things turned out. When I eventually started to get physically better, I became depressed. This was not what I was expecting at all. What I finally figured out was that the reason I was not feeling better emotionally was that I was not dealing with the primary emotional cause of my physical pain – the issues in our marriage. During my year on the floor, Keiko and I had pretty much just stopped being a married couple. Keiko had become my nurse. From my perspective, all of our underlying marital issues were still there and unresolved.

Our immediate and overriding challenge, however, was our finances. As a result of all the medical bills that I had incurred, coupled with my disability insurance payments coming to an end, we would soon be at risk of defaulting on our mortgage. So we decided to sell our house, but we soon discovered that the housing bubble had burst. Six months earlier there would have been people lined up to buy it; now there were none. Once we put our house on the market, Keiko had to close her childcare business at our home. She managed to find another job, but her wages were not enough for us to keep our house.

One morning at the kitchen table, Keiko suddenly suggested something that took me completely by surprise. She offered to go to Japan for a while with the kids where she could work for a much higher wage to help support the family and I could spend some time alone to figure myself out. In the end we decided that she would take our younger son and a book project to work on in Japan and our older boy would stay with me.

Due to logistical issues, it ended up taking another 4 months before they were actually able to leave. So instead of moving on with our lives at that point, Keiko and I got to spend the next four months sleeping in the same bed after we had decided to separate. Although uncomfortable and painful, I believe this was ultimately a very good thing for our divorce process and post-marriage relationship. It forced us to work through many things that we would have just left buried and unexplored if our original plans had worked out.

While Zach (our youngest) and Keiko were in Japan, I managed to sell our home and David and I moved into a duplex. I started working again and began dating for the first time in 18 years. When Keiko and Zach returned from Japan, they moved into the duplex with us. I gave Keiko the bedroom and slept on the floor in my home office. Thus began the most difficult and painful period of our relationship.

Keiko seemed completely miserable. She was forced to give up her home-based pre-school when we sold the house and I was not comfortable with her starting it up again in the small living space of our duplex. Keiko started working as an assistant Kindergarten teacher, but her pay was not enough for her to become independent from me. Becoming a single mom in a country that was not her own, with no family to help her except for me, was a very hard experience. All of her anger, resentment and frustration that she had held in during her time in Japan started coming out – all aimed at me. I felt responsible and guilty. I also still cared for her as my friend and the mother of our children. So, I accepted all the responsibility. I surrendered to being emotionally beat up on a daily basis. I felt like I was doing penance for my sins and that I deserved whatever I got. I just could not stand feeling that I was responsible for her unhappiness, and I truly wanted her to feel better, but there was nothing I could do except allow her to go through her process.

It was not until Keiko was able to establish her business again and move into her own place that we were able to begin healing and move on with our lives. Around this time, we started to talk about a legal separation. Keiko and I both wanted to get separated without dealing with lawyers or court. I sincerely told her that she could have anything that she wanted. I was truly willing to just walk away with nothing – as if a cleansing fire had burned up everything we owned. An interesting thing happened when I shared this with her. Our discussion transformed from a negotiation into a conversation in which both of us were primarily concerned about being fair with each other.

Once Keiko got back on her own feet, she went to a mediator for a legal separation, and I agreed with the offered terms. A few years later, before Keiko bought her own house, we signed our final divorce papers. During this entire ordeal, we have managed to stay great co-parenting partners. To this day, our kids go back and forth between our houses with their stuff and sometimes even with our "shared" Kirby vacuum cleaner in tow!

—⊶⊶⊷⊷—

It is important to note that it is not why we ended up getting divorced or specifically what events took place during that process that is most relevant to creating a Good Divorce, but rather HOW we consciously chose to treat each other during and after this process.

This is true for ALL divorcing couples!

Because we chose to treat each other with dignity and respect despite the inevitable hurt feelings, anger, and resentment we felt – AND because we consistently put the needs of our children before our own, we were able to create a Good Divorce that left our kids undamaged, our friendship in place, and our family assets (what little we had left at that point) largely intact.

So this is what our older son, David, had to say about our divorce process in one of his college application essays:

"When my parents decided to get divorced, I was stunned and speechless. Yet, I was eventually able to understand that a divorce was in the best interest of our family. Going into their divorce, my parents made an agreement with each other to put my brother and my well being before their personal issues. To their credit, my parents have done a terrific job of sorting out their differences and have made sure to be there for us. My parents have had the best divorce I have ever witnessed or heard of. Thus, my brother and I have been able to live a normal life, a life that has not been disturbed by ugly court hearings and arguments.

My parent's relationship is so healthy that Zach and I often forget that my parents were ever married or divorced. For the past five years, my parents have lived in separate homes about five minutes from each other. Even though they are divorced, we have gone on several vacations together and gotten together for family events.

The way my parents have handled their divorce has had a huge impact on my life. The divorce has given me insight into the sacrifice and compromises that it takes to have a successful relationship. Experiencing the healthy and respectful way that my parents handled their divorce has helped me improve my own communication and relationship skills with my teachers, coaches, girlfriend, friends, and family. They were able to role model for us how to end a relationship with dignity and grace."

Chapter 4

TODAY'S TYPICAL DIVORCE: A TRAGIC TALE

(Becky's Story)

Unfortunately, most divorces today are not like Andy and Keiko's. The following composite story is more representative of the kind of divorce that I have observed or heard about when couples do not follow the Good Divorce process.

⊙∞∞⊙

Susan had waited a long time to find just the right man. She did not want to rush into anything. She was determined to find her one and only love. When Bruce drove into town and whisked her off her feet in a flash, she knew it was too late to put the brakes on. With his charismatic style and charming personality, it took no time for her to be drawn into the ease of conversation. He was the dream she had been waiting for.

Twenty years later, that dream came shattering down around her like thousands of shards of glass. Bruce explained to Susan that it had nothing to do with her. His love for her would always be present. Nonetheless, they could not go on living at war, with battle after battle, leaving the retreating lovers devastated and lonely in their own corners of the world. Susan wondered, "Where had she gone wrong?" She was the admired wife by so many husbands, with a well kept home, kids whose politeness most parents drooled over, and a volunteer who made a difference in the community. She and Bruce presumably had the perfect life.

Why then, if it was so perfect, did Susan and Bruce avoid one another for days? The innocent fights of yesterday were now raging storms of hatred, and the easiest way to get through any day was to lay a wide berth around each other. Trust was diminishing by the day, and Susan knew she had to protect herself and her kids. She had seen friends at this crossroads before. And it was the one who administered the first blow that had the power! Susan knew what she had to do.

Several days later, Susan sat in a lawyer's office, a referral from a girlfriend, who said that he was the only person who could protect her now. Susan heedlessly handed over her freedom to "Mr. Right-Along." Of course, she was the victim in this situation as her lawyer had told her. Draining the savings account, she anxiously wrote a $7,000 retainer fee to her lawyer.

Six months later, when the lawyer said that she would be divorced and on her way to a new life, she was instead once again sitting in the courtroom and watching her entire future go down the drain, while the arrogance of the lawyers putting on their show in front of the judge, cost her a "measly" $300 an hour. She kept telling herself that the earlier days of wanting to get back at Bruce were good enough reasons for where they had found themselves. Now she was starting to question her decision. Bruce had tried to convince her that they should use a more amicable route through a mediator, but her fear had put all her faith and her money in the hands of this lawyer, who was now out to benefit himself more than her.

This was her new reality: tougher battles than she and Bruce had ever had at home, with their lives publicly exposed, and a constant grating on raw emotions that never seemed to end. As if she were experiencing a nightmare, she tried to pinch herself to wake up. She didn't awake, though, and the judge ended the session by saying they would be back in 60 days for a new trial. More court? Why couldn't we just sit down and hash this out in one sitting?

⸺⧂⧂⧂⸺

This is today's tragic tale of modern divorce gone wrong.

Susan is caught up in a big working machine with no escape in sight, and the ongoing drudge through endless waiting days, sleepless nights, and deep shadows under her eyes in the morning. She bargained with the devil and gratefully handed over her freedom for his protection. As with most bargains with the devil, you never know what you are going to get.

In her case, she had learned about the inside of a courtroom. She now knew how the wheels of the system moved like molasses, as they creaked their way through number after number. She was not a person, just a case file and number, amongst thousands of case numbers to come before and more to come after. The lawyer fees had long ago exhausted her savings, and now she was working two jobs to keep up with the mounting bills. The house that she and Bruce had once cherished was going into foreclosure, so on top of the stress of the court proceedings, she had to worry about where she and the kids would go.

No one understood. They did not understand how the system set them up to be enemies forever after. Her hope of someday being friends was a small dot on a map, a small island floating on the horizon, beyond her reach. Her friends, who had once reinforced her anger toward Bruce, were now staying at arm's distance, weary of her whining and complaining.

And the kids – she had learned too late that it was not divorce itself that hurt them, but the way she and Bruce handled the conflict that resulted from the divorce. They had utterly failed their kids. She envisioned the little eyes that peered over the couch, wide with fright, as she and Bruce screamed at each other about who was most to blame.

———— ❦ ————

After court one day, Susan retired to her office to grade her student's papers and found that her desk was so buried with piles of divorce paperwork that she could not even enjoy the one haven that she had created. She sat staring at the child custody papers and the transcripts that rambled on and on about why Bruce wasn't a good parent, and what Susan had done to make the kids not like her. It was so ridiculous. Was her freedom worth this?

She thought, "What if I hadn't let my fear get in the way of Bruce and me working this out in a more civil fashion? What if the mature mother who could have chosen a different path for her kids had squashed the thoughts of revenge building in her mind? What if she had chosen freedom over protection, and trusted in her own self-worth to get her through? How different things could have been."

Chapter 5

THE SYSTEM - PLAYING THE GAME

Imagine for a moment that you find yourself having to play a game you had never played before. This game has very high stakes. The outcome will impact your family's financial, physical, and emotional health for years to come. You really don't want to play, but somehow you have to. Some of your friends have played this game or talked about it, but you have never personally played, nor are you very knowledgeable about the rules. Well, it's amazing how many people approach the "game" of divorce – a game that can have devastating consequences to your family's well-being – with little or no preparation.

Many people enter the divorce game without the most basic understanding of how to play. Many people have no idea that the divorce game can be played in many different ways. Most people would be surprised to learn that the divorce game is most effectively played as a team sport with you and your spouse on the same team!

And if you play it this way, you actually get to make up your own rules!

Andy and his ex-wife decided to play the game this way. They chose to raise their kids together as divorced co-parents with no formalized rules or restrictions. They decide things on a week-by-week basis and have been doing this successfully for over five years. They did not hire lawyers, did not go to court, except to file papers, and only paid about $400 for their divorce. Becky's divorce was very similar in experience, including how co-parenting works with her kids.

Most people would be astonished to learn that if there is a true opponent in the divorce game, it is often not your spouse, but rather the Family Law System itself. If you choose to play by its rules, then the courtroom is your field of battle. Does anyone really "win" this kind of fight?

Are any of your friends who played out their divorce on the courtroom "battlefield" happy or satisfied with the outcome?

Wouldn't it be a good idea to learn as much about the Family Law System as you can and about the different options you have BEFORE you start playing the divorce game by someone else's rules?

Conflict Resolution and the Cult of the Individual

Before we start talking about the family law system itself, it is helpful to visit the topic of conflict resolution and the lack of conflict resolution skills in our society. In today's world, one of the most fundamental skills that every person should be taught is the skill of managing conflict. While there are more programs available to educate people on conflict resolution, our society still has a very long way to go.

So, why conflict resolution skills?

First, the better couples manage conflict, the more likely they are to avoid marriage breakdown in the first place. Second, with strong conflict resolution skills, divorcing couples can utilize these skills to move through all the steps needed to create a Good Divorce. Third, it's not divorce that damages kids, it's how the parents handle conflict during and after the divorce process that most impacts their children negatively or positively.

As Andy's son wrote in his college essay, the graceful way in which his parents handled conflict within their divorce process had a very positive impact on his ability to handle conflict in his own relationships. This is a powerful counter example to Myth #3, that kids will be damaged by divorce. It's just not true, unless you and your spouse decide to handle the divorce in a way that is damaging to your kids.

Mediation is a great alternative for many people, and most divorcing couples do come in with basic cooperation skills and a desire to be cooperative. However, what is sorely lacking in most cases is an understanding of the rules of how to play "fair" in mediation, an ability to manage one's internal self-conflict, and an ability to keep the big picture in mind – that maintaining a healthy relationship with your soon-to-be ex is the primary goal.

Beyond our society's failure to teach people how to manage conflict, our traditional values have failed us miserably in guiding us through the divorce process. The result is unnecessary chaos in the lives of many divorcing families.

While our culture puts great value on independence, we often see this taken to the extreme where protecting the rights of the individual becomes the number one priority. People should know their rights and be able to use these as a guide in their decision-making process, but our divorce system has allowed people to throw common sense and teamwork out the window by encouraging self-centeredness. Even the age-old saying, "I'm doing it for the kids" is not really about the kids for the most part; it is more often a way for a person to use the kids to get more of what he or she wants.

Like Andy, I (Becky) have been through a divorce, and my ex and I never had to worry about "doing right by the kids." We managed our divorce as a team, and because of the teamwork approach the natural outcome was that the kids' needs were handled. Did we have conflict? Sure, we had conflict. But, we consistently go back to our common goal of raising healthy happy kids, and that supersedes the need for one of us to feel we have to protect our own interests.

Now, this is not meant to downplay abusive situations. That is a very different story. Without going into too much detail, if you're in an abusive situation, we recommend you seek consultation now. You need to know your options both inside and outside of the legal system.

The Family Law System - The Good

If you are in position to utilize mediation, we are biased in saying that mediation or doing it yourself is a better option than hiring lawyers and going to court. However, since I (Becky) serve many legal document clients, it would be completely unrealistic for me to say that everyone should avoid the court system. Unfortunately, there are just some people who don't have the level of emotional maturity to cooperate. Thus, the family law court system is still the appropriate option for some.

For example, let's say you have a significant other, perhaps you were not even married, but you have a child. You thought you could work amicably outside the court system to come to resolution. Then, one day, the mother goes to Child Support Services and claims that the father spends very little time with his child in order to get more money out of the support system. Unbeknownst to her, "the system" will now go after the father to reclaim that money, whether or not he spends more time with his child. What can the father do?

The father can access the court system to ensure that his time with his child and his income are documented. That way when a decision is made about the child support amount, it is done fairly. In a case like this, having the court system decide the outcome is better than getting lost in a child support system that has no end.

What is the court process in a case like this? The father must take steps to petition the court for help with establishing custody, visitation, and support. There's lots of paperwork to fill out, which is beyond the scope of this book. That is where self-help books like Nolo Press, legal document specialists, and/or lawyers come in as needed. However, the first step is for the father to petition the court. He and his ex-girlfriend will go to court mediation to get the schedule documented, they will submit their financials, and they will get a hearing for a judge to determine final custody, visitation, and support amounts. This will take several months and maneuvering through a maze of paperwork and court procedures.

Unfortunately this maze is unavoidable, because once the child support services action is initiated, it can be very hard to go back in time. In this example, we are thankful there is a solution to help both parties understand their alternatives.

The Family Law System - The Bad

Everyone has to submit paperwork to the courts, but that does not mean you necessarily have to GO TO court. Nonetheless, if you choose to go to court, be ready!

Court paperwork was not intended to be user-friendly, but rather to make people hire lawyers! And to that end, the legal system is very successful. But, the paperwork is just the beginning. Should you not settle with your spouse on your own, use a mediator, or hire a lawyer who settles outside of court, you are going to find yourself in a public courtroom with all your personal dirty laundry hanging out to dry on public record.

Mediation inside the courts is minimal at best. In some places, you will get more time for a mediator to evaluate your situation, but I have heard some horror stories of kids' destinies being determined in a 30-minute conversation. One party might not even get a turn to talk. Are you over-protective of your kids? Tread cautiously. You might "care" too much, and the court will give more time to your spouse, because you have come across as too controlling. Bottom line: do you want to leave your family's future in the hands of someone who does not even know you?

You have some assets – shouldn't be too hard to settle in court, right? But, you have had to "lawyer up" because of all the reasons previously mentioned. Judges do help facilitate moving settlements along, but when you have two lawyers arguing for every piece of property, the ability to give and take is diminished. You didn't even want that boat, and now you are paying your lawyer $1000 to argue over a $600 boat.

The court is a passive entity, which means you have to know what motions and orders to file in order to get your day in court. Divorces do not just happen magically because you have passed a "waiting" period. Everything in court is tied to a motion that is tied to an order, which is eventually tied to what you hope are two parties taking action on the judges' decision.

The Consequences

Anyone who has been in the Family Court System warns others to avoid the system. So why do so many divorcing couples end up in court if no one recommends it and they have a choice in the matter?

Well, what typically happens is that each party lawyers up to make sure that their "rights" are protected. Then, the lawyers begin their arguments about who is more right according to the law. It is true that the law can help protect people's rights, yet when you use the law as a weapon against your spouse, the game is lost from the beginning.

There are lawyers who can negotiate fairly and get an agreement done outside of court. However, proceed cautiously. Being clear where you are willing to give and take will provide the lawyer with the direction to settle, not escalate to court. If this does not happen, then you will inevitably end up in court, with the risk of arguing over more than you ever imagined. As identified in Myth #1, you do not have to "lawyer up", nor do you have to go to court. There are other options that will enable you to get legal advice without having to go through the painfully escalating process of our court system.

Oh, and did you walk into court with some dignity intact?

Unfortunately, you probably will not be walking out the same way. I have sat and observed people belittled, judged, shut down, and worse. We are not here to blame anyone. We are here to tell you that court should be your LAST resort. Do everything you can to talk, mediate, negotiate, and get self-help assistance. When you get frustrated and want to throw your hands up in the air, stop and remember that if you put your life in the hands of "The System" believing that your rights will be looked after, you may have other more important rights taken away.

And how can children not become embroiled in the stress of the court process? They cannot. It is emotionally devastating to all parties. They will feel the stress of both parents fighting for themselves. In most cases, there is no one there to coach the parents through what putting your child in the middle looks like.

However, if you choose to mediate outside of court, you can choose a co-parenting expert who can help you through the process. This co-parenting coach can point out ways children are put in the middle and how the divorcing parties can work together to ensure the kids' emotional needs are managed appropriately. This is a good way to ensure that you are managing Myth #3 by educating yourselves on ways to keep the kids out of the middle and working together to have a positive impact on the kids. It really is possible to instill adaptation, conflict management, and other valuable skills in your kids through the divorce process.

I've seen so many clients almost end up in court because of fear. However, once the client works through the fear, sanity often settles back in, and we are able to mediate to resolution just fine. Do not let your fear run you into a situation you will regret later on. Do not believe you are going to be protected. If you have a lawyer that can make better arguments, you might get what you think you want, but that lawyer will probably cost you twice as much as the value of what you got.

Making a Different Choice

We would never suggest that you go through any divorce process uneducated. Get legal advice, and familiarize yourself with the laws in your state. Then, find a mediator who can facilitate fairness in your particular situation. What works is different for every family. Do not be corralled in to a "one way fits all" approach. Know that give and take is necessary within any process you use. Do not let anyone tell you otherwise.

So what if you are already in the system?

There is no getting out, right? Wrong! At any time, you can both choose to remove yourselves, and find a way that works for you. Many people spend tens of thousands of dollars to finally say, "Enough is enough." You might think you are almost at the finish line, but it's an expensive bet to make. Even the easiest of settlements can turn into a long-drawn out battle within the courts. Why would it not? You have been pitted against your spouse in open court with self-serving lawyers on each side. What did you expect would happen? You thought that maybe someday you and your spouse could be civil enough to be in the same room. You may have destroyed your chance at that. Walk away!

The bottom line question you need to ask yourself is: what if you could avoid all the chaos, drain, and belittlement within the court system?

You can ... it's called CHOICE!

Chapter 6

MEDIATORS & LAWYERS

One of the most important, if not the most important factors in creating a Good Divorce, is that all parties involved are committed to creating the best possible outcome for the "Family System." "All parties involved" include the parents, the children, extended family – and all parties supporting the divorcing couple in the divorce process. When divorcing parties are pitted against each other in an effort to win, gain advantage or extract revenge, the Family System will inevitably suffer in the process. A good outcome is very unlikely in this case.

A mediator's job is to help create the best possible outcome for the Family System. In mediation, there is only one mediator who serves the entire family team. Ideally, there is no winning or losing side when a mediator is used since both sides are on the same team. Of course, the use of a mediator does not guarantee a best-case outcome, but it is much more likely to happen when a skilled mediator is used in an appropriate manner in the process.

On the other hand, in our legal system, a lawyer's job is to maximize the benefit of his or her client. In a divorce case there are generally two lawyers – one representing the interests of each party, each trying to gain advantage at the expense of the other party. A divorce using lawyers is by its very nature adversarial. Each side is trying to win for their client. Yet, more often than not, everyone ends up losing, except of course, the lawyers whose fees increase in proportion to the level of discord they often help to create.

When you use lawyers to manage your divorce process, your divorce often ends up looking like a boxing match with each "fighter's" trainer (lawyer) sitting in his or her corner of the ring (court). Round after round of sparring takes place in which various strategies and tactics are utilized in an attempt to win the fight. If there is no knockout punch, then a split decision leading to a rematch is the likely outcome – an outcome that benefits both lawyers financially, but is often devastating to the finances of the Family System.

Of course, there are situations in which the use of a lawyer is appropriate and prudent. These will be discussed. However, choosing an appropriate lawyer and managing the lawyer's role is critical to producing a Good Divorce.

Mediation

Mediation is still a young field, wrought with good intentions, and still misunderstood by many. Our society is still very litigation-focused, with the focus placed on righting the wrongs of the world. And there are definitely wrongs that need to be addressed in the world, but is litigation the best approach for divorce and family conflict?

In most cases, we believe that it is not.

So what exactly is mediation and why is it preferable to the legal system for settling most divorces?

Mediation is a method of conflict reduction and resolution, which facilitates decision-making with facts, while addressing hurt feelings that surface through the process. A mediator is the facilitator who guides the conflicting parties to reach fair decisions while creating space where the parties can learn to engage their feelings in a way that does not negatively impact the goals of the mediation. Mediation has these major outcomes:

1. Creates an environment where differences can be managed in a healthy way resulting in minimization of conflict.

2. Draws out each person's thoughts and feelings, while challenging people to grow through the process.

3. Provides a mechanism for laying out the facts, while using techniques to minimize the influence of feelings on the outcome.

4. Uses a framework that helps the parties understand how fairness is defined from a "big picture" standpoint.

In its purest form, a mediator needs to be neutral. This means he or she is not favoring either party. An effective mediator should be less in "talking" mode, and more in the space of listening, summarizing, and asking questions. However, that does not mean a mediator does not speak up when something important is being left out, or if a certain level of expertise is needed to bring a fact to the surface. It is the mediator who speaks for the Family System. This should not be confused as bias or a lack of neutrality.

———— ∞ ————

Lawyers

Earlier we said we would answer the question about when family conflict is best handled via lawyers. So, when is it appropriate to use lawyers and the court system?

In mediation: As discussed, the most effective way to utilize a lawyer is to make sure that clients are informed of their rights. Clients can seek a consultation from a lawyer independently of their mediator. Lawyers can write "unprivileged" opinion letters about specific topics sharing their interpretation of a specific law as applied to a person's specific situation. An unprivileged letter means that the client gives the lawyer permission to write his or her opinion about a specific situation.

In cases of abuse: Physical abuse cases are often not good candidates for mediation, especially if there are restraining orders. It does not mean it cannot be done, because mediators can use a form of "caucus" mediation where clients are kept separated physically while the mediator goes back and forth between the clients. However, cases with physical abuse usually mean there is an extreme imbalance of power. Sometimes, a mediator can help to balance that power, and sometimes not. With an extreme imbalance of power, the person who is often dominated will need a lawyer to balance the power.

In cases of wanting everything legal: If one or both of the divorcing parties insist on everything being done by the book, then a lawyer might be the better route to go. The lawyer will ensure everything is done according to the law. In mediation, there is more flexibility. There are some things that have to be followed within the family law system. But, case law is often created from cases with famous people, much of which does not apply to the "average" person. However, there are times when people just want the lawyers and the judge to drive their decisions according to the law. These people would be best served using lawyers.

In cases of mental illness: In extreme cases of mental illness, using a lawyer is probably the appropriate choice. Examples would include paranoia, two narcissists going through divorce, or schizophrenia.

In cases of extreme stalling: There are times when one person really doesn't want a divorce and they stall in any way they can, preventing the divorce from happening. There's nothing to say that a lawyer can prevent stalling any better than a mediator, because the legal system can be utilized very well to stall. However, in combination, legal advice can move a mediation process along by stopping arguments that aren't necessary. Once a lawyer provides a clear opinion on the law   and a mediator is able to utilize that legal opinion to move the mediation process forward, disagreements can dissipate easily. At times, using two lawyers (most likely kept outside of court) could allow for more authority to move a "stalled" divorce through to conclusion.

As you make your decision about using a lawyer or a mediator, it is useful to know and remember the pitfalls involved in either approach.

Mediation Pitfalls

1. If you do not have a mediator who can be neutral, and look after the big picture, then the mediation will not result in a fair outcome for the Family System. If you have a mediator who pushes for agreement without asking tough questions, then you are only getting compromise with little ability to work toward a win/win outcome. If you have a mediator who cannot balance an unbalanced power situation, then mediation is not likely to be effective.

2. Mediators should encourage clients to seek legal advice, provide an educational venue where a lawyer overviews their rights, and/or allow for legal opinion letters in the process. If this is not part of the process, there is no assurance that clients will understand when they are signing off on their rights.

3. You get what you pay for in mediation. You want a mediator who understands how to move people through a process, who knows enough about taxes to refer you to an accountant as needed, who is well versed in pensions, and who can guide you through co-parenting issues if you have kids, and more.

Lawyer/Court Pitfalls

1. Some lawyers will push you to make decisions you do not feel comfortable with and may be trying to create more conflict, which translates into more money for them.

2. Using a lawyer and going to court means that your divorce will have a more devastating financial impact on your family. Our experience is that everything you "fight" for costs twice what it is worth once you get lawyers and/or the court involved. Is it really worth the money?

3. Lawyers are there to represent you (to "protect" you), but if they are not flexible in moving the process along by giving in on some things, while taking on other things, you are going to be in the divorce process a long time and at great cost. If you do not feel comfortable with something, stand your ground or find another lawyer who will listen to and follow what you want.

4. If you are encouraged to seize control of the kids, even though your kids have a good relationship with the other parent, the lawyer is not looking out for the best interests of the Family System. Kids need both parents, and unless there is abuse, neglect, or abandonment involved, the lawyer should not encourage you to fight for more time with your children, when they need access to both parents.

Summary

In mediation, the parties are in control of their own destinies. While some may think that having a lawyer will protect them and thus put them in control, that's not what usually happens. If each party has a lawyer, and that lawyer is fighting for him/her, how can anyone really maintain control? Instead, the lawyers maintain control in their own way.

We do not want to suggest that all lawyers are bad, because there are some very good ones out there. However, the family law system is set up to create more adversity, not less. The timeline drags on and on, and the bills mount on both sides, and the Family System is put through stress for long periods of time.

This is the point where we reiterate that mediation still has a long way to go in being accepted as the best approach for divorce and family conflict situations in this country. We have been led to believe that lawyers are the default choice, whereas the reverse should be true. Lawyers are best used as a last resort, and/or used to supplement a family's decision in mediation. Our society still has it a little backwards, but we are hopeful that our book will help change that!

Summary of Mediation vs. Litigation

	Mediation	Negotiation/ Litigation
Costs	Average total: $2,000-$15,000	Average total: $40,000
Time to Completion	3-6 months	2 years

	Mediation	Negotiation/ Litigation
Emotional Impact	Cooperative, facilitates communication, reduces stress	Adversarial, little opportunity to address issues, increases stress
Role of law	Legal information provided by mediation, but no legal advice given	Legal advice dictated by lawyers
How Decisions are Made	Clients make the decisions	Judges and attorneys make the decisions
	Sets the stage for future, joint decision-making	Sets the stage for more court hearings to have decisions made by others
Impact on Children	Children are considered as part of the big picture and often long-term agreements about the kids are not made until financial decision-making is complete	Children often become "pawns" in the process
		The court decides the fate of kids, and in order to adjust any orders, you have to go back to court
	Allows for child agreements to be tested and adjusted	

	Mediation	Negotiation/ Litigation
Level of Confidentiality	Discussions are confidential	Court hearings are open to the public
	Usually no court appearances	All detailed financial information is part of the public record
	Note: many mediators are mandated reporters, so any violence or abuse must be reported	
Voluntary Compliance with (child support) agreements	Nationwide around 80%	Nationwide around 40%
Tone/Format of Process	Business-like, but informal. Can be done with couple together in one room, or separate in a caucus mediation approach	Formal, adversarial. Lawyers are negotiating back & forth charging by the quarter hour. Both parties appear in court if agreement is not reached outside of court.

Adapted from http://www.ncrconline.com/Divorce/
MediationVsLitigation.php

Chapter 7

THE UNCOOPERATIVE
SPOUSE

(Contributed By Sonika Tinker)

So how do you create a Good Divorce if your partner is unwilling to cooperate? How do you sustain positivity and cooperation when your partner is overtly hostile and attacking? Is it even possible to create a Good Divorce with an unwilling partner?

Yes, it is possible. All things are possible!

There are many tools you can use to successfully turn adversarial situations into mutually satisfying and cooperative ones. You have more influential power than you might think in how your divorce and future relationship unfolds. And if your partner really is and stays unwilling to cooperate in this venture, then maybe you won't have a Good Divorce but you can certainly create a "better" divorce if you follow these principles to the best of your ability.

THE "PULLING" TRAP

Let us begin by talking about one of the biggest traps most people get into when met with resistance by their partners. To begin, bring to mind something you want from your ex that he or she will not give you. Maybe your ex will not agree to a child custody arrangement, or is fighting you on how to divide up property and money, or perhaps you do not like how he or she treats you or your children. Pick one specific something you want and are not getting. For demonstration purposes, let us say you want to receive an additional $400 a month in spousal support and your partner does not want to give it to you.

Now, imagine yourself, literally pulling on your partner's arm, trying to get them to give you what you want. Imagine yourself trying to talk your spouse into it, giving all the reasons why you NEED this money, why you deserve it, and why your partner SHOULD give it to you as you pull. What do you notice? Their resistance – YES! The more you try to get your partner to give you what you want, the less he or she wants to give it to you. Actually, you can pull on just about anybody like that as an experiment and he or she will resist. It is Newton's Third Law of Motion: For every action, there is an equal and opposite reaction. The more you want, the more you pull – and the more you pull, the more resistance you create, and the more resistance you experience, the less you get, and the less you get, the more you want.

Herein lies the trap. The more your partner does not cooperate with your wishes, most likely, the more you try to change him or her. You may argue, plead, explain, attack, nag, withdraw, punish, guilt-trip, cry, yell, and whatever else you can think of to get them to come to your side of things. But in the end, all you do is produce more resistance and unwillingness with these tactics. In fact, the more you pull, the less likely you are to ever get what you want because the act itself actually perpetuates the very resistance you are fighting against.

Take a moment to think about what you are wanting from your partner that he or she is resisting. Another way to ask this is: "What do you want that you are not getting?" Make a list. Do not censor. Whatever you want is okay. Here are some examples: child support, to work things out with a mediator, to spend every Christmas together as a family, or to keep your kids from watching violent movies.

When finished, set your list aside (we will come back to it here in a bit).

So how do you change an uncooperative ex into a cooperative one without triggering all this resistance and tension?

To answer this, allow yourself to go back to your image of pulling on your partner. Notice that the harder you pull, the more your spouse resists. Good. Now, imagine yourself stepping in toward your partner. Notice that the tension between you stops as the pull is reduced. After you step in, let go of your ex altogether and imagine yourself turning to stand alongside your ex, looking in the same direction as he or she looks. Notice that in this image, there is no tension – there is no pulling and no resistance. There is actually some semblance of partnership. Instead of trying to get your ex to come to your side, you merely stop pulling for what you want.

You stop fighting and join them on their side. Bingo. Resistance stopped; in one move.

As we have pointed out in numerous places in this book, the first image of pulling and resistance is the dynamic that is created and exacerbated when you use lawyers to manage your divorce. The second image of standing side-by-side working together is the dynamic that is created when you are on the same "team" managing the divorce process using a mediator.

Now do not worry, this does not mean you have to go along with everything your spouse wants. But it does mean that you have to quit pulling on your partner if you want to quit creating resistance to what you want. To produce cooperation, you need to expand yourself to include your partner's needs, concerns and point of view. You need to see things from their side just as much as you want them to see things from yours. You need to be willing to look at what he or she wants and what YOU are willing to give, just like you want them to give you want YOU want. As Gandhi said, "Be the change you wish to see in the world." Simply put, deal with an uncooperative spouse by changing yourself first. When you change you, you cannot help but positively impact the situation. Now, you have the secret to transforming Myth #2. You can undertake mediation even if you do not trust your spouse because all you have to do is be the first one to give a little trust. Then, you will get a little in return, and the rebuilding of trust can start.

To do that, however, you need to understand a couple of things.

Your ex is not fighting YOU. Your ex is not AGAINST YOU. This person is not out to GET YOU. Your ex is FOR himself or herself. You ex is just trying to take care of some need or concern of his or her own, just like you are.

When you think of your partner as being an obstacle to you getting what you want, there is a tendency to think of him or her as the enemy. This view of your partner as the "problem" will spark feelings of victimization and powerlessness, and the moves you make from this stance will only reinforce resistance and lack of cooperation. Instead, think of your partner as someone just like you, with legitimate needs and concerns that he or she is trying to take care of. Allow yourself to be curious about what those needs might be. Perhaps she wants to make sure she will be taken care of financially? Maybe he doesn't want to be told what to do and wants to feel in control? Maybe she is afraid of losing contact with the kids? Perhaps he doesn't want his quality of life impacted by having two houses to be responsible for?

When you connect to the needs and desires of your spouse, it opens up the door to finding common ground. As already stated, a Good Divorce is predicated on taking care of everybody's needs and desires as best as possible and creatively coming up with win-win solutions. You cannot creatively problem-solve if you do not know what your partner's concerns are – so you have to slow things down enough to find out why your partner wants you to pay that extra $400 a month or why she does not want you to have every other weekend with the kids. What is the real need or concern behind that push for talking to the kids every day or keeping the boat that you bought last year? Surprisingly, as you ask questions and listen, you may discover that your partner's needs are very similar to yours.

You don't want to struggle financially or lose contact with the kids either – even if you cannot agree yet on exactly how you are going to mutually take care of these needs. This understanding of your partner's concerns is a crucial step to creating win-wins in the short run and a Good Divorce in the long run.

There are a couple of ways to find out your partner's concerns. One is to simply ask questions in a genuine mood of curiosity. "Can you tell me what you imagine would happen if I had the kids every other weekend?" "Can you tell me why you don't want to give me this extra $400 a month?" "Can you share with me what this $400 means to you?" Questions like this will elicit the needs and concerns of your ex and will point to the issues that need to be addressed in the solutions you propose.

If communication has really broken down and you cannot have this kind of conversation with your ex, another way to get at your partner's concerns is to role-play with a good friend. Have your friend role-play your ex, and with you role-playing yourself, argue about a real issue in your relationship. Argue for "why" you should get what you want. Address what you are trying to take care of in your argument. Your friend will hopefully be doing the same from your ex's point of view. Listen for the concerns as you engage in the role-play situation. After a few moments, switch roles. This time argue your ex's point of view against "yourself." As you do this, you will find yourself better able to step into your ex's world and access his or her positive desires and intentions.

As you explore both your own concerns and those of your partner, you may be surprised at the answers. For example, you might say that an extra $400 a month means you can keep your current job and still pay for your son's monthly medical expenses. Your spouse might say that he or she wants this $400 a month to go into your family health savings account to pay for medical needs. What at first seemed like opposition, now reveals commonality – you both want this money reserved for medical expenses. This information paves the way for creatively coming up with a solution that satisfies both of you.

But let us say you discover your partner wants this extra $400 a month for his golf membership and you want it for your son's medical expenses. It could be easy in an example like this to think that your partner is being selfish while you are trying to take care of the family. In all fairness, let us assume all concerns are created equal. Taking care of your son's medical expenses so he can be healthy and vibrant and you can feel relaxed is as important as your partner taking care of his own health and relaxation by socializing and exercising on the golf course. Even here, you can see that you both value health and you both want to be relaxed. It is also probably true, as you look deeper, that your partner shares your concern for your son's health, just as you share your partner's concern for taking care of your own body and your social needs. Even here, in what appears to be conflicting desires and concerns, there are shared concerns underneath your diverse wants.

Once you understand your concerns and the concerns of your partner, put them up next to yours. Write out what you both want, what you are both wanting to take care of and what you are both wanting to experience. "We want to take care of our son's medical expenses. We want our son to be healthy. We want to enjoy ourselves with friends. We want to do things we love, like play golf. We want to feel healthy and good. We want to feel relaxed."

Can you notice the different mood produced when you look for where you are similar versus where you are different? Can you see the possibility for working things out together from here?

Next comes the fun part, sometimes the most challenging part, and that is to ask, "What resolution can I come up with that will take care of BOTH of us?" Your cooperative solutions need to be able to creatively address ALL concerns – both yours AND your partner's.

When you ask this question, your mind will begin to search out an answer – an answer that addresses BOTH of your concerns. Answers that would not have shown up otherwise will begin to appear. For example, you might decide to get a different health insurance plan that takes better care of your son for less money. Or maybe he will shift down to four times a month for golf instead of 12. If you get stuck or have a hard time coming up with alternative solutions that would work to take care of both your concerns, seek out a friend or mediator to help you come up with ideas. Because a mediator or a third party is not attached to anything in particular, they can often help you think of options you have not thought of.

TO-DO ACTIVITIES

1. Make a list of what you want. Have your ex-partner do the same thing.

2. Take each item and ask yourself: "Why do I want what I want? What concern or need do I imagine that 'something' will take care of?"

3. For each item your partner wants, ask him or her the same question, "Why do you want that? What concern or need

will that take care of for you?" If you cannot talk to your ex, role-play with a friend to help you "guess" what their concerns and needs might be.

4. Make a list now of all the concerns and needs you both have.

5. Creatively come up with solutions that will allow you both to get all, or as many as possible, of your concerns and needs met.

GIVING FIRST

When you are in a stalemate in your relationship, or you are producing hostility, defensiveness or resistance in your partner, it is usually because you are trying to get something. Focusing on "getting" is the same energetic move as "pulling." When both people are trying to get something from the other, and nobody gives, unfortunately, nothing moves.

One way to get things moving is to give first. And if you want to get things moving quickly, give fast.

To give to your ex, you need to first put yourself in a "giving" mindset, which to be honest, may be difficult if you have been fighting a lot. But remember, he or she wants something good, too. Your ex wants to be given to as much as you want to be given to. When you give, he or she can lower his or her guard and feel more relaxed about giving back to you. Once again, you now have the secret to rebuilding trust, allowing you to squash the myth that you cannot utilize mediation because there is no trust. Trust is a matter of perception, and you have the power to impact that perception by giving first.

This is the secret that Andy discovered when he had the inspiration to offer his wife anything she wanted in their divorce mediation. As he said, this completely changed the dynamic from a negotiation into a conversation with both parties more concerned about fairness than in getting "theirs."

I (Sonika) remember one of the highlights of my divorce, was my three-year-old daughter sitting at the counter while my ex and I divided up kitchen items. She glanced up at some point during the process and said, "You two are sharing very nicely!" I believe our willingness to give to each other rippled out and positively influenced our children in our divorce – they actually felt given to in the divorce! They now had TWO great houses to live in, for example, instead of only one. Giving fast and giving first not only role models for our spouse and kids how we want to be treated, but feels great and sets the stage for mutual give and take arrangements in the future.

So sit down and explore what you are willing to give to your partner to take care of his or her concerns. What would feel good to you to give? Sometimes asking questions, like, "What would best serve the children?" or "What would challenge me to grow the most?" can help you find something to give.

TO-DO ACTIVITIES

1. Write down what you know your ex is wanting from you.

2. Put an asterisk by the items you are willing to GIVE to your partner.

3. Think especially about what you are willing to give that means a great deal to them and would feel GREAT to you.

AGREEMENT FRAME

When your partner disagrees with you in conversation or does not want to give you something you want, your first response is likely some defensive or offensive reaction. Perhaps you feel shocked, hurt or angry and you lash out or withdraw in response. There is another great tool you can use at these times to help reduce tension in a hostile situation: the "Agreement Frame."

The Agreement Frame is a linguistic tool that you can use to verbally pace your partner and then lead them to where you want the communication to go. The agreement frame is basically a set of words that you say to energetically "join" or agree with your partner before adding in your own thinking. Phrases include, "I can see why you might say that…" or "I understand that…" or "I agree with you…" or "I appreciate…" or "I respect that…"

How it works is that when your partner says something, especially something you have a strong reaction to, you say one of the above listed phrases (i.e., "I respect that and…"). Once you have agreed with your partner and shown understanding, THEN and only then, you add in your own thinking. You do that by adding an "and" at the end of your sentence. For example, "I respect that you want to have the kid's every Christmas, AND I really want to celebrate that special holiday with them sometimes, too." Do not use the word "but" at the end of your agreement statement, as

---

that tends to negate the first thing you said. To say, "I respect that you want to have the kids every Christmas, BUT I really want to celebrate that special holiday with them sometimes, too" implies opposition. When you use the word AND, you expand to include both of your desires in the same sentence.

This way of communicating will amazingly and quickly disarm opposition and create more harmony in your conversations with your partner. Try it and notice what happens.

TO-DO ACTIVITIES

Next time you talk to your spouse, use the Agreement Frame:

I agree … and …

I appreciate … and …

I respect … and …

MIRRORING

Another way to shift out of pulling and sparking resistance and uncooperativeness in your spouse is to see them as your mirror. One of the things I have discovered in my work with couples, is that everything – every quality, habit, trait – you despise, resist or appreciate about your ex, also lives in you.

Now, when you want to end your relationship with someone who drives you crazy, the last thing you want to believe is that you are like this person. But believe me, there is nothing more powerful than humbly acknowledging your own inadequacies and inefficiencies. You are human and fallible, just like everyone else. No one is perfect. And no one exhibits only one side of any quality. We are all selfish AND generous. We are all self-centered AND caring. We are all patient in some areas AND impatient in others.

We are all a little bit of everything.

The people you admire and those that drive you crazy are mirroring back to you aspects of yourself that you cannot otherwise so easily see.

When you can look squarely at yourself and own these mirrored aspects, the tension and upset between you and your partner can evaporate into thin air. Imagine actually feeling compassion and love for your spouse instead of exasperation and frustration? The shift between you and your partner that will arise from looking in the mirror at yourself will have profound, positive and lasting ripple effects.

There are usually two sides to looking in the "mirror."

One is to see where you are just like this quality you do not like. This is usually a shadowed aspect of yourself that you do not own or see. A great way to look in the mirror is to think of a quality your partner has that you cannot stand and ask, "How am I just like that?" You can use the title of this chapter as a place to start: my partner is uncooperative. Now ask yourself, "How am I just like that? Where and how am I un-cooperative?" With an open mind and genuine willingness to explore and see the truth, you will begin to see many ways in which you are also uncooperative. Without judgment, just allow these ways to present them as they float into your mind. Remember, we are ALL uncooperative from time to time – anybody on the planet looking for where they are not cooperative would be able to see it. Notice how you feel as you tell the truth about your OWN lack of cooperation. As your own unwillingness to cooperate sneaks out from behind the shadows, you are likely to feel some compassion arise as you discover that you are just like your partner.

Sometimes looking in the mirror is not a straightforward comparison, so it is harder to see where we are just like this quality. For example, I used to judge my ex for being messy. At first, I didn't think this "mirror" exercise applied to me, because I am clean and orderly. But when I looked further, I got to see that I made a mess of my relationships by often trying to keep the house perfectly clean. I became angry when clothes were left out on the floor or the kitchen was not cleaned up. In that way, I was also messy. So, if at first you cannot see where the mirror applies, broaden your scope.

Another side to looking in the mirror is to explore how more of this quality might be GOOD for you. Often, you push away qualities that would actually have a positive benefit for you. For example, my ex was able to ignore dirty dishes and play with the kids, which I envied. I too wanted the freedom to not be held hostage by chores and to play more! I wanted to be just as "at choice" about where I put my attention and time. In that way, the mess of my ex was mirroring for me my inability to make other choices that might have been more fulfilling and fun for me, too.

Once you have looked in the mirror of your partner to see yourself, you may find yourself feeling a bit more accepting of your partner's flaws and negative characteristics. Looking in the mirror at ourselves is a powerful way to reduce or eliminate tension and judgment. The act of taking qualities we hate and feel victimized by, turning them around, and using them to see and grow ourselves, is a "power" move.

Instead of your partner's behaviors affecting YOU negatively and throwing you into reaction and a "victim" stance, you can shift your attention onto your OWN behaviors – often the only place you truly have the power to change.

Just like we talked about in Chapter 1, operating within your circle of influence rather than from your circle of concern is one of the keys to creating a Good Divorce.

Looking in the mirror is also a LOVE move. Instead of producing separation by believing you are different and better than your partner, your heart softens when you realize that you are really no better at all – you are in fact, just the same.

TO-DO ACTIVITIES

1. Make a list of all the judgments you have about your ex. For example: critical, slob, selfish, etc.

2. Next, look at each item and ask two questions:

   How am I just like that? Tell the truth. For example: Explore where you are critical. Are you criticizing him for being critical? Criticizing yourself?

   How might having more of that quality be GOOD for ME? For example: Maybe you are too nice, do not stand up for yourself, or do not tell the truth about what you think.

————— ∞ —————

SEE THEM AT THEIR BEST

Imagine you could wave a magic wand and your ex would suddenly be loving, kind and cooperative. Who would he or she be if they were their best self? Imagine your partner as this "best self" – centered, wise and mature; open and powerful; or sensible and giving. See them being that way in your mind. This is by far, the most powerful thing you can do in dealing with an uncooperative spouse.

There is a great deal of scientific evidence to support the impact we have on each other with our thoughts. Henry Grayson, a leading psychologist, reports in his book *Mindful Loving* that his alternating positive and negative thoughts about his wife directly influenced their relationship. For two weeks, unbeknownst to his wife, he alternated thinking positive and negative thoughts about his wife and their relationship – one day thinking only positive thoughts, and on the next, only negative. Without fail, on the positive-thinking days, she sweetly greeted him at the door when he arrived home from work and they proceeded to have a lovely intimate evening together. On the negative thinking days, she was nowhere to be found in the house, and when they connected, they inevitably ended up in a spat that lasted into the evening. Upon reconstructing his experiment to his wife, she acknowledged having corresponding positive and negative thoughts about HIM!

These and other experiments point to a deeper truth: our thoughts are CREATIVE in nature. What this means is when you believe your ex is uncooperative, you actually create and support them to keep showing up as uncooperative. And if you focus on where your ex is cooperative and generous and kind, you will actually help your ex to be cooperative, generous and kind. Your thoughts have creative power.

By taking just five minutes a day to see your partner being sweet, cooperative and loving in your mind's eye, you can direct your creative energies toward the realization of these positive qualities in your partner. Do these practices every day for 21 days, and you may well be surprised by how easily your partner seems to change. I have experienced many a miracle in my 35 years of working with couples, where significant behavioral and character changes that seemed impossible before suddenly appeared out of nowhere from this practice alone!

In addition to seeing your partner as his or her best self, focus on his or her positive aspects. Pay attention to what you appreciate about them. Notice what you like. And dare to speak your appreciation out loud. Why? Because what you appreciate, appreciates. What you focus on gets bigger. What you put your attention on, you will see more of. You are creating with your focus of attention – so if you want more cooperation, put your attention on what you wish to see. Besides, when you share what you appreciate, not only will your ex feel better, but you will too. Every time you look for something to appreciate, something to be grateful for, you actually receive what you are appreciating. Herein lies your ability to transform Myth #4 (I will never be able to love again). You receive love for yourself when you give love to others. You give to yourself when you give to someone else.

Another great creative practice is to look for ways in which your partner is already how you would like them to be. Where is your ex already cooperating? Where is your ex taking care of your concerns?

How is your ex expressing generosity and showing a willingness to work things out? Often in relationships, when there is conflict, we tend to narrow our focus to the things we DO NOT like and DO NOT want. We miss out on all the goodness that is ALREADY there. When you shift your focus to what you like, not only will you feel better and more at ease, but your ex will pick up on your shift of focus too. Your ex will relax their defenses in the face of your acknowledgement. Remember everyone wants to feel appreciated and seen as a good person – your ex included. There is no faster way to reduce hostility and inspire cooperation than looking for where your ex is already cooperating and letting them know how much you appreciate his or her effort.

A great side benefit to these practices is you will feel better. Your self-esteem will increase. You will like yourself better. Instead of matching your ex's hostility with your own hostility and becoming exactly like what you are hating, you will sneak your way around into being how you want to be – relaxed, appreciative and peaceful. Not only that, but negative beliefs triggered by your partner's resistance will begin to change. Instead of believing you never get what you want, you will begin to see that you do in fact, get what you want, at least some of the time. These shifts in belief will open the way for you to create a radically different relationship experience for yourself, not just with your ex, but with all your future relationships.

Truthfully, of everything said in this chapter, this is the most important! Do not underestimate the power of your thoughts. See your ex as their best. Focus on their positive aspects and go out of your way to express your appreciation. Believe me. In just five minutes a day focusing on his or her best self, you can expect to see some drastic positive shifts in both of you. Bump up the good results several notches by looking for and expressing what you are grateful for, and allow the goodness of these feelings to take on a life of their own. Let this practice spill over onto everyone you encounter – your kids, in-laws, mediators, friends and associates. You cannot help but create a better divorce for you and your family by engaging in the regular practice of looking for and expressing appreciation for the many blessings you are receiving right now.

TO-DO ACTIVITIES

1. Take five minutes a day to focus on the positive aspects of your ex. See him or her as his or her BEST self!

2. Write down what you appreciate about your ex. Where IS your ex cooperating? Where IS your ex helping out?

3. Pay attention to what you appreciate. Notice what you like. Speak your appreciations and express your gratitude aloud.

———⸺———

IT'S ALL GOOD!

What is really great about dealing with an uncooperative spouse, no matter how you slice it, is you will grow as a person. You have the opportunity to mature, expand, and develop yourself. Let's face it. It beats the "miserable victim" alternative by a long shot!

So go into this experience knowing "it is all good." You are going to be a much stronger person out of this experience. Consciously use your challenging experience deliberately to build your center, power, clarity, alignment, compassion, understanding and love. Become the person you have always wanted to be.

The practices in this chapter will help you to shift your experience with your uncooperative spouse. Remember to be gentle with yourself. Mastery will not happen overnight. None of us received relationship training in school. You have been engaging in some pretty unworkable relationship patterns for a long time. These practices will take awhile to take hold. Just do your best and keep practicing. Ask for help when you need it. Do not feel you have to do this alone. Get support. Find a relationship coach. We all do better with people rooting us on and showing us a better way.

Rest assured, as you steadily incorporate these new practices, take responsibility, change your outlook and focus on a more positive one, you cannot help but to positively influence your divorce experience.

Chapter 8

FINANCIALS: ASSETS, LIABILITIES, & SUPPORT

Every relationship gains assets along the way. Couples invest in stocks and bonds, buy houses and cars, and purchase expensive "toys." The inevitable acquisition of material items also leads to the accrual of liabilities. When divorce happens, one of the biggest challenges is how to divide assets and liabilities – and this can be one of the biggest decisions outside of how to co-parent minor children (if there are any).

Many people come to a mediator with an idea of how they want to divide things up without consideration for the numbers or what is considered fair. Say I will keep my car and you keep your car, yet you do not realize that your car has negative equity while mine has positive equity. I have decided that I won't touch your retirement, because I have my own accounts. But you don't realize the difference in the value of the accounts because I have a 401K at face value of $50,000, while you have a pension that does not reflect on the

statement what it is really worth. There is actually a difference of
$150,000, and you had no idea that kind of gap existed. If both par-
ties are working together to come to an agreement, you can decide
almost anything you want. However, it is useful to have a neutral
party asking the questions not thought of.

(Please note: this is not considered legal advice. If you want
advice on how actual family laws are applied, you should seek the
opinion of an attorney.)

THE PROCESS

The biggest mistake that most divorcing couples make is to mix
up the process of valuing and dividing assets and liabilities. If you
want to create a Good Divorce, it is imperative that you follow these
3 steps in the following order:

1. Identify all the marital assets and liabilities

2. Research and agree on the value of all the assets and
   liabilities

3. Divide the assets and liabilities in a fair way (and don't go
   back to step 2!)

NEVER MIX THESE UP!

Marital Home

Key Questions:

Is there a marital home?

What is owed on the home?

What is the value of the home?

Let us start with the marital home. What is the current mortgage statement balance at time of separation? Have you agreed on a value either by running a "Zillow[4]," getting an informed appraisal, or requesting a formal appraisal? The parties should decide who is keeping the house. If there is equity in the house, it is easy to plug that positive number into the balance sheet. If there is negative equity, then things get a little more complicated. Are the parties going to short sale the house? Is one party going to take on the house? If one party is going to take on the house, what is the liability worth? Will that person assume all the liability? What happens if he/she cannot assume liability based on lack of income or good credit?

These are all questions that need to be answered - with help from an expert if needed.

Vehicles

Key Questions:

What vehicles have we purchased during our marriage?

What do we owe on the vehicle/s, and what is the private party Blue Book value?

Do we both agree on the condition selected of the car in the blue book evaluation?

---

[4] http://www.zillow.com

After the marital home, it is easiest to identify the vehicles. What are the cars, trucks, RVs and/or boats owned? Were these acquired during marriage or before/after separation? What was owed on the vehicle at the time of separation? What is the Blue Book private value amount? The difference between the Blue Book and what is owed is the number that is used to determine worth.

Investments

Key Questions:

Do we have investments such as stocks, bonds, CDs?

How much are these worth?

Using the statement immediately following your official date of separation, record the face value of the stocks. You can find the value of Savings Bonds online at treasurydirect.com as of the current date.

Bank accounts can be more complex. The simplest, most straightforward way to handle your joint bank accounts is to split the balance 50/50 and put the money in separate accounts as soon as it is feasible.

If one person pays the bills acquired during marriage, but after the bank accounts are separated, then he or she should get paid back half when the overall picture is reconciled. Another option is to divide up who is paying what bills.

What happens if one person was the stay-at-home parent, and does not have income? Then, child and spousal support can be used to pay 50 percent of the bills. Sometimes, 50 percent of the marital bills and support cancel each other out. Sometimes, one person owes the other (again not literally, but figured into the whole pie). The important point is that a line in the sand is drawn, and from that point forward support is paid and marital bills are split 50/50.

Retirement Accounts

Key Questions:

What are all our retirement accounts?

Did we acquire or add to these accounts while we were married?

Are we comparing apples to apples such as 401Ks that are pre-tax and ROTH IRAs that are post-tax?

What is the pension worth if we have one?

Retirement accounts can be the most tricky of all the assets for three major reasons (a) you often need to look back at prior employers to ensure you did not leave a retirement account behind, (b) rarely will a pension system inform you what your pension is worth in order to evaluate it as part of the asset total, and (c) you need to have a general understanding of the different types of retirement accounts (i.e., ROTH IRAs have already been taxed, but traditional IRAs have not).

It's easy to get statements for regular retirement accounts at date of separation. Use the face value of the accounts. If you have ROTH IRAs in the mix, you need to consider that a ROTH IRA is worth more since taxes will not be taken out in the future. You cannot know what your retirement accounts will be taxed in the future, but expect to add roughly 15 percent average to a ROTH IRAs current worth. There is no perfect way to do this because it will also depend on who takes the traditional retirement and what tax bracket they may find themselves in the future.

Pensions need to be evaluated. If your company does not give estimates of the total asset value, find someone who will. Pay to have it done. The pension is the most underestimated asset in most cases. If you are going to split the account 50/50, then it is not as important to value it.

In pensions, pre-marital amounts are part of the overall calculation. Regular retirement accounts are not so easy. The easiest way to handle this is to find a statement the month before marriage and subtract it from the statement at date of separation. Another way could be to take the total value and divide by how long it's been open, multiply by the years of marriage, and use that figure (i.e. $100,000/10 x 5 yrs marriage = $50,000 marital). Again, this is not a perfect science, but you need a rough way to value the assets before and after.

These are all questions that need to be answered - with help from an expert if needed.

Home Contents

Key Questions:

Have we distributed home contents 50/50? Otherwise, arguments will entail about how much each party kept.

Do we value items at yard sale price? But, you kept the majority of the items, and I had to buy new things at full price…how is that fair?

Usually, it is logical to most people that everything sells at market value. That is the reality because you have a yard sale and the purchased price is market value. However, if one person takes the majority of the contents, then the other person will need to buy new things. So, the fairest thing to do is to split the contents 50/50 or to find a combination of yard sale pricing and replacement costs that makes the person "buying" as whole as possible.

If one person is moving to a smaller place, you can still split the contents 50/50, and additional items could be sold at a garage sale, put on consignment, or have an estate sale representative take the items off your hands for a fee (most likely lower than market value).

Taxes

Key Questions:

Have back taxes been included in the overall financial picture?

What is being done with any tax refund or liability from the time before we separated?

If there are back taxes owed, the fairest thing to do is to split them 50/50. It does not matter who accrued them. There are many arguments around back taxes, because each party has justification for "who" should pay. In a situation where one person was the breadwinner, and the other person a homemaker, and the back taxes cannot be equalized with other assets (i.e., the breadwinner keeping more of the retirement in exchange for paying the taxes), then 50/50 is the way to go. Either way, make sure the taxes are paid off by one person immediately or split by both parties. The government is going to hold you both responsible, and there is no way around this one.

What if your separation date did not come until the half-year mark, but your divorce is final and you will be filing individually on your taxes? The months you were together should be considered, and any tax refund or liability accounted for in some way. You can account for this in the agreement by saying that any tax refund or liability of either party will be split 50/50 after the total liability is divided by 12 and then multiplied by the months before separation (i.e. $5,000 liability/12 months x 3 months together in the year =$1250 liability to split 50/50).

If you are going to be divorced by the end of the year, have you considered changing your exemptions on your W-4? You will most likely end up with fewer exemptions, so you need to re-look at the exemptions you are claiming for payroll.

Liabilities

Key Questions:

How much debt do we have and how are we going to split it?

Can we offset debt with any assets so the lower breadwinner does not run into cash flow issues?

As with taxes, if debt was accrued, it's a 50/50 split. You can talk with a lawyer or accountant about an "innocent-spouse" clause if you didn't know about the debt. Typically, though, you are responsible for 50/50.

Businesses

Key Questions:

Are there businesses, and how are we going to get them valued?

Businesses come in all sizes and types. Some are worth getting valued, others are not. Many times, such as in consulting businesses the income produced is going to be used to calculate support. In these cases, one has to be careful to not "double dip." I have seen many business owners threaten to walk away and close down their business rather than pay out an amount for the business and then still have to pay support. If the business is easy to close down, and start backup, this may be an indicator of its worth. If the business has products and inventory, it is going to be hard to avoid a business valuation.

Use good common sense and logic. Determine if a business valuation makes sense. A valuation could cost more than the business is worth. Look at the facts, and then determine the best course of action.

VALUING ITEMS

As emphasized earlier in this chapter, the best practice for valuing items is to identify all the items and agree on their values before you ever discuss who gets what. Many items, but not all, should be valued at time of separation. Use common sense to agree on items that cannot be valued at the time of separation.

For example, has a particular liability been paid by one party after separation (this person should get credit for those payments against the value set)? Has there been enough of an increase or decrease in a retirement account that the account would now be valued negatively if split in two?

Regardless of how it's done, it's important to agree on the values first.

DIVIDING ASSETS AND LIABILITIES

Once the values are agreed to, then and only then should the parties determine who will take what. Once the values are set, you should not go back to revalue items.

At this point, a spreadsheet can be used to place items under each party. A total of assets minus liabilities should be tallied all the way down each column for each party. If there is a difference on one party's side, additional assets/liabilities need to be moved, and/or one person will pay out an "equalization" payment to get the balance sheet to 50/50.

―――――∞∞∞―――――

CHILD SUPPORT

Usually, child support is fairly straightforward, unless parents play games by using the children as pawns to manipulate the outcome. This section is focused on a privately, mediated outcome and will not address support determined by the courts.

Once parents have a set schedule, then support can be calculated. Most mediators use a software program to plug in numbers such as the parents' incomes, co-parenting time in a percent, health insurance costs, daycare costs, etc. Nonetheless, child support is an algebraic formula that can be hand-calculated if you are so inclined.

With child support, the higher earner will pay the lower earner even if time is shared 50/50. This is to ensure that each parent can provide for the children financially at a similar level. Child support technically belongs to the child, although the parent receiving support is making decisions on how to spend the money. Child support covers the basic necessities of shelter, food, transportation, clothing and health.

Extraordinary expenses are those things that parents pay above and beyond the basics for things such as extracurricular activities or medical needs not covered by insurance. Again, this information is not intended to be legal advice, as the law might deal with things differently depending on where you live. We typically mediate extraordinary expenses pro-rata, proportional to the amount of income each party has. This is determined by taking the income of the lower earner divided by the total earnings of both parties to get a percent of what each parent pays. Child support is included in the lower earner's income before this ratio is calculated. Extraordinary expenses should be agreed-to by both parties ahead of time in order for reimbursement to be paid out with educated consent.

SPOUSAL SUPPORT

Unlike child support, spousal support is much more complex and one of the most contentious areas of a divorce settlement. In particular, this is often a place where the parties will choose to get legal advice before deciding on a number together. Because of the strong legal implications of spousal support, we will not be covering this topic extensively.

Nonetheless, we find it important to say that regardless of what your rights are around spousal support, the lower earner should work towards self-sufficiency as quickly as possible. There are too many unknowns in this world to rely on your ex-spouse for your financial stability. That being said, the higher earner should still have the higher level of fiduciary responsibility while the lower earner transitions to a space of financial self-sufficiency. This does not happen overnight; it takes time.

DRAWING AGREEMENTS BACK INTO A SUMMARY

The divorce plan starts with translating agreements into a plan. It is important to understand the family code language that is required by the courts in your county. Financial assets and liabilities should be listed in a "facts" section and detail every account number (at least the last four digits) and value in this section. Once the facts are clearly stated, then you move on to summarizing the agreements. There are many templates out there on the Internet. Make sure you get one that is within your state, and even better your county. Otherwise, you could end up missing key information required for your jurisdiction. Check out our website for additional resources.

Note: It is important to know that the information in this chapter is not legal advice. The approaches we use are based on fairness that is defined by my (Becky) experience over time, customized to each client. If you want the legal way to approach division, you will need to seek legal consultation.

Chapter 9

THE KIDS

"Nothing affects the life of a child as much as the unlived lives of its parents."

~ Carl Jung

There are a lot of people who stay together for the sake of the children. We do not doubt that people have the best intentions for their children, but there is another benefit of staying together: You do not have to deal with the unknown, loneliness or challenges of being a single parent. So, the boldest question of all is:

"Will your unlived life be the model you want for your children to have for their own adult lives?"

Kids are more resilient than you might think and each one acts very differently. Some will be devastated and want their parents to stay together. Others will be so tired of the fighting that the relief of not having to hear the fighting anymore is the greatest gift they could be given. Some children will thrive with the new opportunities and experiences presented to them because of the divorce. No matter, there are approaches that can aide kids in a healthy transition, just as there are behaviors that can create lasting damage.

Which side of the coin would you like to be on?

Despite all my (Becky) poor experiences with divorce in childhood, what I do know is that I would not be the authentic leader who takes the world for a spin into a transformational direction if I had not experienced my parent's divorce. You see I was quite shy as a child. I hardly talked. I was deathly afraid of the playground. I preferred to read on my own and make up worlds that fit my image of what could be. I am not even sure what a shy, quiet and in-her-head-type of a person I would have been had my stepdad not come along.

So, in spite of the negative impacts that divorce had on me, I was also given great gifts. I was given the gift of voice. I was given the gift of full expression and the ability to stand up for myself. I learned how to interact with people more comfortably. In one summary sentence, I can say that I transformed from a girl who would hide in her cave all day long to a woman who could deliver a presentation to hundreds of people with confidence, purpose and fearlessness. I got access to a second chance!

Recall Andy's story as well and the college essay that his son wrote on the gifts he received from the way his parents handled their divorce process; sometimes divorce can actually be beneficial to children!

With this in mind, let's get started at your new business – the business of raising great children together as divorced co-parents.

First, we would like you to imagine that you, your ex, and your children are on a riverboat for a journey. Imagine this journey will not end until your child becomes 18, even after you get divorced. If you have more than one child, this process continues until the youngest child becomes 18. These tips are your way to ensure you flip Myth #3 (getting divorced will damage your children) on its head. You have a choice in how your kids turn out during and after your divorce!

On this journey, you will find yourself frustrated with the same things that led to your marriage breakdown. You may want to sever all ties and try to minimize any interaction with your co-parent. Your former spouse may try to pressure your kids for information about your new life. Regardless of the ups and downs, you made a commitment to your children, and while co-parenting is different from parenting, it is hardly less important. The techniques to be presented here are tried-and-true ways of minimizing the negative impact of your divorce on your kids.

Tip #1: Don't have conversations/arguments about the kids when they are present.

Fighting in front of your children will cause them to take on blame for your situation, and that's the last thing they need in an already unstable time. If you need to correct your spouse or disagree with him or her, do it later. Your #1 job is to create a sense of security that mom and dad are adult enough to interact respectfully with each other. This goes for in-person and phone conversations. Children know when a co-parent is on the other end of the phone.

Tip #2: Don't put your kids in the middle.

Don't transfer messages from one parent to the other through your children. The kids may forget to give the message, and the delivering parent could then be upset with the child. This is not fair to the child. In addition, the receiving parent could have a reaction to the message that the child might take personally. Parents need to step up to the plate and deal with communication directly, no matter how tough. The good news in today's age is that we have e-mail and text messaging, which can make communicating with each other easier.

Tip #3: Kids need to understand they have two homes.

Many times one parent stays in the marital home, and the other parent moves out. For the one who has left, that parent is always going to battle the accidental and purposeful language that kids will use when they refer to home. As a co-parent who left the marital home, I (Becky) had to reiterate for years that home is where mommy and her girls are. And it was an unfortunate set of circumstances that I had to move three times in a 1.5-year period, so what the girls called home beyond dad's house was very confusing.

So, we had to redefine the concept of home. Home is where the family is. We even emphasized traveling back and forth between two homes to be an adventure. Traveling is an important value of mine, so we could find adventure in any type of travel. Car time can be quality time for parents and their children.

Tip #4: Don't lay your emotional burdens on your children.

Use support groups, friends, counselors, etc. for emotional support, not your kids. Children, no matter what age, should not be a substitute for a good counselor or other adult support. This does not mean that co-parents can't talk about the divorce with their children. Kids need to talk about their feelings too. And kids are intuitive! Whether you think they know or not, they sense what is going on. So do not ignore the issues. But do not try to satisfy your own emotional needs through your children. Rather, focus on taking care of the emotional needs of your kids.

Tip #5: The family can take advantage of this time to enhance the skill set of transition and adaptation.

In today's world, there is no better skill than being able to adapt to changing times. Our world moves at high speed, and there is rapid change in motion every day. Divorce provides an opportunity for you to increase your skills of flexibility and adaptation – and provides an opportunity for your kids to learn to adapt from your example. When I (Becky) was young and we had to move multiple times due to my family's divorce situation, it was overwhelming, discouraging, and in many ways paralyzing for me. But each time, I learned to adapt more quickly. Today, I thrive during change and transition, and I am able to help others adapt through transition. There has never been a more highly used skill set for me than that of adaptation. Think what your kids can learn for future transitions. Change never stops!

Tip #6: Don't make decisions about the kids in court.

The court is not a place where children's destinies are best determined. There are cases, in particular with a parent who has a mental dysfunction, when the courts need to be utilized. But if at all possible, don't do it. Putting decisions about your children in the hands of someone who does not know your life, does not know your children's lives, and gets little time/information to make informed decisions can be a huge mistake you are stuck with for the rest of your life.

Imagine sitting in a meeting with someone for less than an hour, after which time they write up a recommendation to the judge about what should happen with your kids. Or worse, you go through extensive and expensive assessment mediation where your entire life is aired in reports and court appearances. Believe us, you do not want to put your family's lives in the hands of someone else!

Tip #7: Be cautious about comparing your situation to others.

Every co-parenting situation has a very different outcome. Parenting styles are different. Working schedules are different. Distances between parents homes vary. Today, even primary caretakers are different because there are so many more men taking an active role in parenting. The diversity of parenting plans is extremely high. Accommodations for the developmental stage of the children must also be considered. Each parenting plan needs to be customized to meet the unique needs of each family.

Tip #8: Children need access to both parents. Speak well of each other to your children.

Who has not had a fleeting thought along the way that it would just be easier to snatch your kids and go off with them into your own world? I (Becky) know I have had that thought. What stopped me? No matter how critical my ex and I could be of one another, I knew that my children loved their dad, and there was no replacement for him. My new husband is a wonderful dad, and my kids love him dearly, but he's still not "their" dad. There is just no one like Mom, and no one like Dad, even with all the flaws that come with them. So be sure that your children have access to both parents.

It is also very important to speak well of your ex to others, and especially to your children. Otherwise, your children may feel they need to pick sides and choose loyalties. This will put them in the middle of your conflict and potentially alienate them from one or both parents. Instead, focus on nurturing and supporting your children's relationship with BOTH parents. This is one place where that saying, "Do unto others as you would have them do unto you" really bears repeating. You would want your ex to treat you respectfully in front of the children, to not damage your relationship with them, so give the same courtesy back. Don't let your negative feelings towards your ex ruin your relationship with your children.

As often as possible, provide a united front of love focused on your children, so they can have the best possible relationship with both of you.

Tip #9: Finish the financial settlement before you make permanent decisions about the kids.

If you run your decisions about finances either before or in parallel with your decisions about your kids, they are bound to become pawns in the game of winning or losing. You need an interim plan, but your interim plan should start out mostly status quo, and it should evolve over time to move closer to a 50/50 time share. Until financials are settled, nothing should be set in stone. This way the kids are not used as pawns in the financial negotiations.

Tip #10: Figure out as co-parents what things are co-parenting business and what things are not.

One of the most difficult things that we can put our kids through is putting them in a position to "tattle" on Mom or Dad. Even the most innocent questions can be a burden for a child who only wants both parents to love him or her. I have seen the worst kind of inquisition happen to a child who wanted to spend less time with his dad to avoid the barrage of questions about mom every time he was with him.

Even when the children tell you about things happening at the other co-parent's home, it is a good idea to get in the habit of saying, "Thanks for sharing, but I do not need to know what your Dad is doing." Unless there is a safety threat, things that happen at Mom's house should stay at Mom's house, and things that happen at Dad's house should stay at Dad's house. Co-parents do not need to be monitoring the other parent's dating situation or any other personal topics that are no longer the business of the ex. There is a fine line between co-parenting business and business that is not relevant to co-parenting.

Co-Parenting is for Life

The business of raising good kids takes a lot of practice, patience and perseverance. The reason you left your co-parent is because you grew apart, could not communicate well, or fought all the time. But now, you still have to raise kids together. The moment you committed to bringing kids into the world (or adopting kids), was the moment you committed to raising those kids together with your co-parent for the rest of their lives (or at least until they are of an age to take care of themselves).

Maintaining a positive relationship as you raise children together is crucial for the success of your family in the long run. The truth is you will be joined for a lifetime through your mutual commitment to the well being of your children.

Chapter 10

CHOOSING YOUR TEAM

The people you surround yourself with can make a huge difference in the quality of your life. In divorce, this becomes even more important. Those who are in your corner will play a pivotal role in supporting you in creating a Good Divorce.

We like to refer to the people you surround yourself with to support you during your divorce as your "Divorce Team." Making it through a divorce involves so many moving parts that it is critical to make sure the people on your team are people you can trust and count on. And while you might think you do not need support, we have found that your support team is one of the most important success factors in creating a Good Divorce.

How to find the right team Members

Imagine you are the hiring manager at a large company and you need to hire a new financial controller. How would you go about this task?

Would you.....

- Rely solely on the recommendation of friends and family?

- Use the yellow pages or an Internet search?

- Hire the first person who walked in the door?

- Hire someone without checking references or getting testimonials from other employers or clients?

Or would you...

- Seek referrals from qualified sources

- Check references and get testimonials from trusted friends or colleagues who could PERSONALLY attest to the quality of the person's work

- Interview several candidates for the job with a set of thoughtful questions

We hope that you chose list number #2. But, it's amazing how many people choose professional Divorce Team members according to list number #1. Do not be one of those people!

As we talked about in Chapter 1, how you go about choosing your divorce team members is something that is completely within your circle of influence and will have one of the biggest impacts on the quality of your divorce process as well as the outcome.

But what happens when one of your team members is not working out?

If a team member is not working out, you need to talk to that person and express your feelings of dissatisfaction. Often giving feedback to your team member can create a quick change in behavior without having to reinvest in finding a new team member. However, if a person on your personal Divorce Team is negative and toxic in your life, making a break from that person can lead to a more positive outcome.

If a professional member of your team is not working out, you can replace that person with someone else who will better support your needs.

Sometimes there are on-going personality conflicts with someone on your team. If feedback has not worked, and you have exhausted your options in helping this team member understand your needs, then it's time to find someone else.

Creating a Good Divorce requires a Good Divorce team!

———— ✁ ————

So now that you know why and how to build your Divorce Team, where do you start?

Friends & Family

The most important place to start is with your immediate friends and family. You need friends and family members who will be supportive of what is right for you and your family. But be cautious. The most seemingly helpful friends might be deceiving. If your friend is not supporting the Good Divorce process, for example, if she is telling you to "screw your spouse," she is not the right friend for your support team.

You need friends who are focused on helping you grieve your loss, let go of the past, and focus on the future. It is these friends who will support you in moving beyond Myth #4 that you cannot love again. You can and will love again, but part of that transition requires surrounding yourself with people who bring the right energy to your mutually shared space. Negative energy is toxic. Family members should be non-judgmental and support you in your decision to move on. Anyone who cannot do these things should be distanced until you can move through your divorce.

Once you have enlisted family members and friends who are looking out for your family system as a whole, you should select professionals who are going to help facilitate your divorce.

Mediator

There are different types of mediators, and you will want to consider what flavor of mediator will fit your situation best. There are some mediators who believe that every session with your spouse should be done together in the same room. This perspective is fine, although, that is not how it HAS to be done. In divorce sometimes by the time you are done with each other, the last thing you want to do is spend every meeting in the same room together.

My (Becky) firm's process allows for "caucus" mediation, which means that meetings can be done separately. This does take a highly skilled mediator who can be neutral, hold the big picture, and ensure that both parties feel like they are getting the best of the mediator.

Lawyer

As discussed, a lawyer should be a compliment to the mediator, giving legal advice where it is needed. You do not need a lawyer to handle every piece of your case. Find your mediator first, and then see what recommendations he or she has for lawyers who believe in the Good Divorce process.

You will want a lawyer who is going to look at the case from the big picture, while giving you the legal advice you need to ensure you have weighed the pros and cons. We have mentioned some specific examples throughout this book of areas where you might want to understand your rights. But, keep in mind that ultimately you are in charge, and you want to accept the feedback given based on what fits your situation best.

Counselor/Divorce Coach

The last main team member to consider is a counselor for you and even possibly your kids. If you hesitate to do counseling, consider a divorce coach. Or you can empower yourself in other ways through self-growth courses or support groups.

Having a resource on your team to support your emotional transition can make the difference in how long you are "stuck." Everyone goes through a transition. Transitions involve going through a similar phase of feelings, such as shock, anger, resistance, understanding, exploration, and commitment to a new path. Unfortunately, we have seen people who are stuck for decades after a divorce in anger, and they cannot move on to find a new partner, take care of themselves, or find happiness. The type of support you get while you are in the divorce process can help you to move on to your brighter future sooner. It will move you along your path to being loved and to loving again, shooting Myth #4 out of the air.

Now that you have assembled your main team: family, friends, divorce facilitator, and professional support group, it is time to determine what kind of extended team members you may need. Here are some ideas about who else may be helpful to have on your Divorce Team.

Accountant

Do you have complex tax issues that an accountant can help answer?

It would be a good idea to have an accountant do your taxes even though you might usually do your taxes yourself. Divorce brings a few more tax complications than you may be used to, so utilizing an accountant your first year in or after your divorce can be very helpful.

Financial Adviser

Are you starting over financially?

If you are starting over financially, you could use the help of a financial planner who will look out for your financial big picture and get you back on track to a sound financial future.

Real Estate Agent

Do you need to sell your house?

Maybe you need to do a short sale? You may need a real estate agent who will work well with both partners and include everyone (including the mediator) in communication about the sale of the house.

Mortgage Broker

If you have equity in your home, and want to refinance, do you have the right mortgage broker who can crunch the numbers and give you multiple options for taking over the home?

If you need to assume liability of the home, ask your current lender about an assumption of liability process. Sometimes, you have to ask the same question in multiple ways to get what you need, especially with your current lender. Current lenders are not incentivized to give you anything they do not have to. It is riskier for them to only have one person on the loan, so be assertive.

House Appraiser

Are you and your spouse trying to come to agreement on the value of your home?

If you do not have a recent refinance appraisal, or an easy way to come to agreement on the value of the home, then perhaps you want to consider an independent appraiser. Be sure to agree before you go into the appraisal that you will accept the appraised value as the value that you will be including in the mediation or negotiation.

Organizer

Do you have years of "stuff" to sort through?

An organizer can get you to that end game much more quickly. He or she will help you assess why you may be holding on to things, why it is important to keep certain things, and what you should do with your stuff once you decide to let it go. Within this category, you might get the aid of an estate sale expert who can help you value your things for an estate sale. Or you might contact your local county for your once- a- year junk dump.

Life Insurance Agent

Do you have kids? Are you paying support?

If so, it is a good idea to get life insurance if you do not have any. Once you agree to life insurance, you should not change your policy, only the percent left to each beneficiary over time. Before you do this, you should be in communication with your ex on any change in the amount.

Estate Planning Attorney

Do you need to update a will or trust? Do you need to create a will or trust that aligns with your divorce decree?

Once the divorce decree is complete, seek the help of an estate-planning attorney to ensure that you have your affairs in order. You should also include what will happen with your kids should something happen to you and/or your spouse.

Bankruptcy Attorney or Debt Counselor

Do you have too much debt to handle now that you are living in two separate households?

It may be helpful for you to consult with a bankruptcy attorney or debt counselor. Keep in mind that you could be responsible for your ex-spouse's debt, so you need to evaluate your options, know your rights, and understand what will happen with all the debt.

Technology Support

Will you be moving? Do you have to set up your new at-home electronics infrastructure?

If this is a frustrating effort for you, consider hiring a tech expert (or a friend) who can get everything set up in a few hours. Save yourself a lot of headache, and get up and running quickly with the right support.

Handyman

Do you need simple repairs done on your house to ready it for sale?

Are you going to be on your own now and need a handyman around to help with the things your ex-spouse used to do?

While money may be tight in the beginning, doing what you are good at yourself, while outsourcing things not in your area of expertise could save you more money in the long run. This assumes that your time is more valuable focused on your job or business.

Movers

Do you need to move?

Movers can be costly, so start putting away for a mover as soon as you know you are going to need to move. Or enlist the help of strong friends and have a moving party day where everyone pitches in to help.

Cleaning Services

If you are selling a home, does it need to be cleaned?

Spending a little money on cleaning can take a lot of stress off the table.

Career Empowerment

Are you looking for a job or considering a career change?

A career empowerment coach can jump start you into a new job or career much more quickly than if you do it on your own. You may be putting out some money up front, but in the long run the shortened time it would take you to get a job could be well worth the initial investment you make.

IMPORTANT THINGS TO DO

In addition to enlisting support resources, there are a number of important tasks we recommend you take care of as part of the Good Divorce process.

Get Your Own Health Insurance

Is your spouse the primary on your health insurance?

After the divorce is final you will not be able to stay on your spouse's health insurance plan. If your spouse works, his/her company has to offer you COBRA, but it's often a costly expense. Using an insurance broker to help you find health insurance can save you money, ensure you get the right type of insurance, and take a lot of stress out of the process.

Update your Auto Insurance Policy

Are you and your spouse already living apart?

Once you and your spouse are in separate residences, updating your auto insurance policy to two separate policies is important. It will probably cost a little more because you may lose your multi-car discount, but not having to argue over who is paying for it, and how much one owes the other, can make it worthwhile to pay a little more. Talk to your insurance agent to determine the best policy for you now that you are on your own.

Get your own Cell Phone Plan

Are you on the same cell phone plan?

If you are, you will need to have the person who is not primary on the account assume the liability of their phone on their own plan.

As long as you stay with the same carrier, contracts usually do not matter. All you are doing is separating the plan into two accounts. It will probably cost more because you will not get the advantage of shared minutes or less monthly fees for secondary users, but at some point, you will want to make the break to your own plan.

Take Care of Yourself

Is your stress level rising exponentially? Do you think about your own self-care?

Going through a divorce is a Top 3 stress producer. Taking care of yourself is critical. Again, while you may not have a lot of money, setting some aside for a gym membership or for a massage, will be worth it in the long run!

Chapter 11

THE DIVORCE PROCESS REVEALED

Now that we have presented everything that might be involved with a divorce, it's time to look at the big picture of the entire divorce process in an organized and systematic way. Many people will say, "I have never been through a divorce. Where do I even start?" This chapter is meant to help guide you in your own decision-making process and action steps.

So, where DO you start?

As with any major change in one's life, before you open a new chapter, it is a good practice to make sure that you have finished the prior chapter. Take a look at the Appendix on assessing potential marriage breakdown. The answers to the questions in this section either lead you to a positive readiness for divorce, or they lead you to additional work to be done on your marriage with your spouse.

Before reading any further it will be helpful to visit our website (www.thegooddivorcebook.com), download our divorce process diagram, and print it out to reference while reading through the rest of this chapter. Each step in the process diagram is labeled and referenced in the text.

DIVORCE METHODS

The first step that you will need to take in the divorce process is to determine the method you will use to divorce. Will you (1) do-it-yourself (2) use mediation or (3) use a lawyer. Do not forget that these methods can also be blended. In order to help you figure out your own personal answer to this question, we have provided a quick and simple Divorce Complexity worksheet on our website. We strongly suggest that you take some time to complete this worksheet before continuing.

Do-it-Yourself

To assess the feasibility of the do-it-yourself process, there are a couple of things that must be in place.

Are you amicable with your ex? This is a requirement for do-it-yourself, because if you two cannot communicate well, you are not going to be able to move through the paperwork process and its necessary steps (1A).

How complex is your divorce?

For every one of the following things that you have, the complexity level (1B) of doing it yourself increases: retirement accounts, kids, debt secured by both of you, back taxes, pre-marital property, large sum gifts or inheritances, a business, a pension (different from retirements). If you have more than 2 or 3 of these items, do-it-yourself is going to be very challenging.

You could still be in the do-it-yourself space if you only need help with one or two items, such as assessing and dividing a pension or designing a co-parenting plan with the help of a professional (1C) who can include all the required items for the courts (1D).

The bottom line: how well do you read instructions and fill out paperwork? Can you figure out the requirements of the court process on your own? The answers to these questions will make do-it-yourself accessible or not.

In most cases, this is the quickest and least expensive method of doing your divorce.

In Andy and Keiko's case, they went the do-it-yourself route while using a mediator to guide them through the paperwork process – in essence, they used a blended approach to produce the most efficient and inexpensive outcome in their particular situation.

Use Mediation

If you cannot do-it-yourself, then your next exploration should be mediation. In mediation, ground rules will be established (2A), and you will be able to create accountability around how you will interact, what will happen with the kids, and what the do's and don'ts are during the process.

During the ground rules process, or soon thereafter, you will develop a detailed list of all financials that need to be disclosed (2B). The mediator will organize the data into an understandable format that will allow you to validate the financials (2C). After that, it's time to mediate the division of the assets and liabilities (2D). Mediation could take anywhere from 2-6 sessions depending on how complex your financials are (2E). In addition, if you have children, there may be additional sessions for co-parenting education, and time to develop a plan for co-parenting your child/ren (2F). Make sure you have completed the financial negotiations before you come up with a finalized co-parenting plan (this will ensure children are not used as pawns in the financial decisions). Once you get agreements, these will be drawn up in a document (2G). At this point, you can have the document reviewed by a lawyer (2H). Or if you got legal advice somewhere in the process, you may feel comfortable with the agreements. It is up to you at this point. Caution, though. Do not let a lawyer draw out the process by not efficiently reviewing your documents and giving you feedback.

In most cases, using a mediator will take more time and cost more than doing it yourself, but should be significantly less expensive than using lawyers.

Use a Lawyer

If you decide to use a lawyer in the traditional way, you will work with your lawyer to determine if you can attain a negotiated settlement out of court (3), or whether you will be going into court to have a judge help settle matters (4).

Negotiated

If you go the negotiated route, you will gather data (3A), organize data (3B), negotiate (3C), and either come to agreement or not (3D). Coming to an agreement may take months and months as lawyers push paperwork back and forth between one another trying to get you what you want. The more people you add to your case, the more expensive and drawn out it gets, because it requires more communication. The petitioner's lawyer talks to the respondent's lawyer who then talks to his/her client, who then re-contacts the petitioner's lawyer to make an offer, and back and forth it goes. Hopefully, you reach a settlement at some point (3E), and your paperwork is filed with the court for dissolution of marriage (3F).

Court

If you cannot work out a negotiated settlement with your spouse, you will end up in court. This is the worst-case scenario and unfortunately, the most common, yet couples do not always know they have a choice. In this scenario, your case gets set for trial (4D). You will then likely attend a settlement conference before you go in front of a judge (4E). If you do not settle in the conference, then your case goes to trial (4F). If you do go to trial, expect a series of settlement conferences and trials that could last for a few months or a few years.

Also, if you have kids and you choose the lawyer route (4A), you will probably end up in court regardless, because it's often mandated in some states that lawyers send their clients through the court child mediation process. In most cases, you will go to a mediation appointment with your ex and a court mediator who listens to both sides, and then writes up a recommendation for your kids (4B). Beware, depending on how impacted your court is, the fate of your kids could be decided in an hour. After the mediation session, your case will go in front of a judge (4C) to finalize custody, visitation, and determine child support, if applicable.

This is by far the most expensive, time consuming, and emotionally damaging path, especially if you have children. And unfortunately, in our current culture, this is the most common outcome. But, now you know better. You are empowered to make different and better choices for yourself and your family.

Chapter 12

MANAGING THE EMOTIONAL TRANSITION

In every transition, a person goes through an emotional process that follows a very similar path to the stages of grief that Kubler-Ross has so eloquently framed. We also find that each person in a couple will go through these stages at different times, with one partner usually further along in the grieving process than the other. This may make it appear like one person is not going through a grieving process, when in fact they probably started the process awhile back.

In our experience, it is important that people go through the grieving process as consciously as possible, although no two people will go through it at the same speed or in the same way. Nonetheless, if ignored, a person can get stuck. Without healing, it may be very difficult for a divorcing person to move on to a new relationship (which makes Myth #4 not a myth at that point in time, because loving and being loved can be more difficult), or he/she might move on to an unhealthy relationship that repeats similar destructive patterns from the past.

Some people may move through a stage in the transition more quickly. Others may think they are moving through the transition completely only to discover later that they need to revisit an earlier stage because it was not actually fully completed.

We would have liked to put this chapter at the beginning of the book, but in our culture, consciously dealing with your emotions is often an afterthought to major change. We do not often see ourselves as conscious creators of where we are going. It is easier to see ourselves as passive bystanders in our lives. It may not feel that way, yet we often do not have the energy to move from passivity to the active participation of creation, especially during stressful times like divorce.

Thus, this chapter has been placed here at the end. These are powerful tools that if applied can make the difference between moving on to happiness or being stuck in years of anger, denial, and bitterness.

Stage I: Marriage Breakdown

This first step of acknowledging that the marriage is in breakdown can be very hard to identify because it usually takes place over a longer period of time. In this stage, there is a lot of fighting, which could include outwardly expressed anger, inwardly expressed frustration, and withdrawal.

If you are in this situation, there can be a lot of confusion about what to do. The hope of the past is still hanging in the air, but it becomes harder and harder to carry that hope forward.

This is the time to get counseling, use the Marriage Breakdown Appendix to assess whether the relationship is at a point of no return, and take workshops that will allow you, as a couple, to come back closer together. This is the time for behavior change: NOW! If you cannot commit, as a couple, to behavior changes, with timelines and ways you can support one another to change, then you risk reaching the point of no return with no opportunity for rekindling or reconciliation.

Stage II: I Have Made the Decision

Since one person is usually further along in the transition curve, it usually means one person has quietly made the dreaded decision to leave before the other. They might have been planning their exit strategy off and on over a period of months, with no real action. Or they might be more actively making decisions on "when," "where," and "how" to go. For the spouse not yet thinking about leaving, this EMOTIONAL part of "I've made a decision" may come only after both parties in the couple have made a decision to proceed with a divorce.

This is often the point in time when there is some relief. Most people dislike being what we call "in limbo." Once a decision has been made, at least we know what direction to face. There is still confusion, and even a bit of shock that this is really happening, but the reality of being without one's spouse is now looming on the horizon.

In this stage, it is important that professionals are sought out who can help you make a clear decision. Being in limbo for too long is not healthy for either spouse. Make a pros/cons list of staying and going and be sure that the side for "going" is longer than the side for "staying." Measure your readiness for leaving using the Marriage Breakdown Appendix as a guide to reinforce your decision to leave. Start to explore what it would take to find out who you are as an individual.

Stage III: Separating Physically and Maybe even Legally

For a lot of people, the first step in a separation is to live apart either in separate locations or in separate bedrooms. This is still a hard time, because it's easy to slip into old routines. The feeling of relief that was starting to wash over you may dissipate as fights still occur. Being in such close proximity within the same house, or even still having your affairs co-mingled makes a clean separation difficult.

At this point, a couple may decide to file court paperwork, seek out professional help, or take some action to move them in the direction of creating a future apart. This is a bittersweet moment as there is some movement towards creating a new future, yet a definite step away from the dreams that were created as a couple.

In this stage, boundaries are critical. If you are trying out a separation period, then make sure it really is a separation, where you are learning to be independent. If you have lingering doubts, then commit to dating again. Start fresh. Take a workshop that will facilitate you leaving the past in the past. Notice whether letting go creates an opening for staying or if the opening for your new life becomes wider.

Stage IV: We Have Made the Decision

Once the couple has come to a place where they both understand the marriage is over, it is still not a clear-cut path to a new future. It is more of a step forward, and a step back, as each person has bouts of denial (step back), then exploration (step forward), then resistance (step back), then picturing one's self in a new life (step forward).

However, in this stage the decision has been made, and the couple is moving on to create new lives. Separation is becoming more and more extensive as names are removed from credit cards, the home is sold or refinanced into one spouse's name, and the kids are going back and forth between two houses. Doubt about the breakup may creep in at points in time, but then recalling the fighting, the lack of intimacy, and the pain of being together rapidly overshadows the doubt. Eventually, the lingering hesitation subsides, and the former couple moves forward into the reality of separation.

Again, in this stage, boundaries are imperative. You have to learn to live on your own before you can have that friendly lunch together. You have to be your own person before you can invite your ex to hang out at a function. Now is not the time to try to be best friends.

It is time to focus on you, and what you need in order to move forward. Take time to grieve. Cry, get angry, and let go of what is not meant to be. Say good-bye to the dreams of your past, and get ready to create the dreams of your future.

If you recall from Andy's story in Chapter 3, it wasn't until Keiko had moved out of their shared apartment into her own place and had secured her own livelihood again, that they could really begin the process of healing and becoming friends again.

Stage V: Exploring Your New Life

Now, each person in the couple is an individual on his/her own, exploring a new life. Each has sought out new relationships, rekindled old friendships, and looked for activities that will be fun and beneficial. This is an unexpected place where a person can get stuck. If you put your toe in the water, and get bitten one too many times, you may just give up. But, this is the worst time to give up, because "stuckness" can grab on to you, and hold you captive for as long as you will let it.

Instead, continue to go out in the world and fight back the fear, the rejection, and the expansiveness of the unknown. Do not let Myth #4 get the best of you. You can love and be loved. Do not let this be the time to run away. The only way to reach a brighter future is through the long trek that includes periods of darkness.

Now is the time to make a list of all the things you wanted to do but did not when you were part of a couple. Create a vision board with pictures and words of all the things you want to create in your new future.

Be real with your budget. Cut out the expenses that are not healthy, and not contributing to your growth. Instead, make space in your budget to save for fun activities, trips, and self-care that will bring you back to remembering the best of who you are.

Take your time dating. Do not jump into another relationship right away. Do the work to be clear on what contributed to your last marriage breakdown. Transform your unhealthy patterns and be clear on what you want from your next partner. Create a list of characteristics of your ideal partner, then redo the list with more realistic expectations. Assess whether you are dating the people who fit your values. Identify the red flags, and keep track of those early on in any relationship. If you see too many red flags, back out quickly. Do not second guess yourself. This is the time to rebuild trust with yourself.

Stage VI: Finding Your Brighter Future

You are standing on the mountain with the sun shining on your face. You have made it! You have a clear vision of your new life, and you are implementing it. This is YOUR time. Make it worth any lost years you may have had, and seize the moments in time to pull yourself into the future.

Continue to revisit your vision. If you created a vision board, keep it posted. Consider creating a second board as you achieve your first vision in order to propel yourself further into your brighter future. Enjoy the present. Celebrate your accomplishments.

Be alive!

Appendix I

ASSESSING WHETHER YOU ARE IN MARRIAGE BREAKDOWN

When people come to seek a divorce, there are so many questions. What happened? Why did our marriage breakdown? If you are assessing whether you are in marriage breakdown, this Appendix will help you figure that out. If one or more of the following sounds like your relationship, seek counseling assistance quickly. There can be a point of no return, where so much damage has occurred that divorce becomes inevitable. Work on these things before it is too late.

Sit down with your spouse and talk over whether these things are issues. If you cannot talk about them, they ARE issues and you need to seek counseling or mediation to help facilitate communication. In many cases, we have had one spouse in a couple who says they never saw it coming. Have you been listening carefully to your spouse? Do you really know their feelings and emotions? It doesn't matter if you are making long-term plans for travel, life insurance, or other future endeavors. A breaking point does not know the future. It knows the present, and that the pain in the present has become too much to bear.

#1 – Communication, Part 1: Respect

Good communication in marriage is respectful. Good communication avoids such disrespect as sarcasm, judgment, and put-downs. Disrespect of your partner causes a slow chiseling away of love and passion. Is your communication respectful, or does it show grave disrespect? Good communication in marriage is a two-way street. Respectful listening is also important. Good communication in marriage is honest. Lying causes long-term consequences to the marriage relationship. Honesty is not merely avoiding falsehood. Honesty also means that we do not avoid sharing information that our spouse has the right to know and would want to know. Good communication also takes time. Spending time together talking and listening can be done in many ways in addition to sitting down face-to-face. How is your communication? Is it respectful or full of disrespect?

#2 – Communication, Part 2: Listening

If you spend a lot of time in your head, you probably are not really hearing your partner. When one partner says, "I did not know anything was wrong," it is usually because they really were not listening. Body language can be even louder than words. If you are not taking time to learn visual cues, and paraphrase back to your partner what you think you heard them say, you are not exhibiting active listening. Do you know how your partner likes to be listened to? Some people like to vent. It is important to hear the underlying message in the venting. Some partners want help resolving an issue. It is important to ask questions, get facts, and brainstorm solutions.

Are you asking your partner what she/he needs in the moment? You can learn a lot from asking, as that is a very important form of listening. How you ask questions is key to getting the person to communicate with you honestly. There is a lot more to listening than you think. How well are you really listening to your partner?

#3 – Commitment

One of the worst things we can do in a relationship is to do things that turn away from or push away our partner. The most critical time to move closer to your spouse is when things are at their most difficult. When you are in a fight, the manner in which you engage with your spouse can be the difference between contributing to marriage breakdown or to building up the marriage. Deadly phrases like "maybe, we should just get a divorce" (while not necessarily meant) are the types of words that contribute to the biggest wounds. Words can build up or tear down. Actions that don't demonstrate commitment can be the biggest contributor to growing apart. Many times, when people say they have grown apart, it is because they have done things over time to put out the flame. What kind of things do you do or say that might be diminishing the demonstrated commitment you have with your partner?

#4 – Making your Partner a Priority

In today's world, we have so many competing priorities. You cannot put everything else in your life before your relationship and expect it to survive. Just because you think your spouse will always be there does not mean they will if you neglect them as a priority. It is the little things that count: the handwritten notes left around the house, greeting your spouse when they get home, or the show of affection every day, several times a day. Romantic gestures can go a long way toward keeping the kindling burning. We hear that everyone is so busy. Do you know where busyness gets you? It gets you to more busyness. You have to take the time out to focus on your partner. Is your partner the number one priority in your life?

#5 – Forgiveness

Forgiveness can sound cliché. However, just because it sounds cliché does not mean it is not imperative. Forgiveness does not mean you are condoning the "wrong," but rather being willing to move on. What is really important is not allowing the power of the emotion behind a grudge to hold you back from an expressive, loving life. Do not forget to forgive yourself as well. Have you forgiven?

If the answer is no, consider this: a lack of forgiveness leads to resentment, bitterness and blaming. These emotions can consume you in ways that are not evident but cause deep roots of pain over time. How do you stop the blame game? What support do you need in order to partake in the ultimate act of forgiveness?

#6 – Infidelity is not Always about Sex

Many things contribute to infidelity, and it is important to keep in mind that infidelity is an indicator that something is not working in one or more parts of the marriage. It is important to look at the range of infidelity, including both physical and emotional forms.

Infidelity is the single most powerful sign of the relationship's dysfunction. When you begin to confide in another person with whom you have an emotional attraction, the risk of attention being diverted from your primary relationship is huge. Who do you confide your deepest emotions to? Are you more attracted to someone else emotionally than your partner? Would you be willing to cut off that personal relationship if asked?

The importance of these questions is not in blaming or placing guilt somewhere, it is about assessing whether you can go back and fix what has contributed to the emotional or physical breakdown with your partner. Is it too late to go back and repair the rifts in your relationship? Only you can answer that question.

#7 – Distractions

Healthy relationships require presence by both parties, and if we are caught up in many distractions by "things" other than our partner, marriage breakdown is likely. These "things" often include text messaging next to your spouse, playing computer and video games in place of spending time with your partner, and obsessing over pornography. It is not a far leap to fill in the blank for yourself. What type of "text time" distracts you from your partner? Can you or your spouse change your behavior to increase talk time?

#8 – Social Media

Facebook is being implicated in over 20 percent of the divorces that take place in the United States (Huffington Post, June 2012). Common Facebook issues include gossip about your partner, rekindling old romances, and flirting with new prospects while married or committed to another. Can you identify any dangers in how you use social media?

Similar to infidelity, Facebook issues are often associated with a breakdown in marriage. Are you utilizing Facebook to avoid your relationship?

#9 – Acceptance

We all have our own personality, our own love language, and our own cultural conditioning. In any relationship, we can either learn to accept and even cherish these differences or try to change the other person. First, it is important for each partner to understand what the differences are. Second, it is critical to talk about how these show up in your relationship. And most importantly, the last step is to learn to accept the person for who they are.

This does not mean you cannot challenge your partner to grow or to stretch beyond their cultural conditioning. But, you have to accept that fundamentally your partner is not going to change. Hopefully, you selected them for who they are, not who they can become. If you want your partner to be the ideal image in your mind, you are not in a lasting relationship. Do you try to change your partner? Is he/she constantly trying to change you?

#10 – Emotional Baggage

Everyone has his or her own emotional baggage. The question is how well you manage that baggage within your relationship. We often select partners who can help us work on our childhood wounds, yet what often happens is that our partner's behaviors just become triggers for expression of the baggage. We expect that the other person will carry our baggage for us. For example, you may be sensitive to criticism, so you expect your partner to walk on eggshells around you. Instead of dealing with our own insecurities, we expect our partner to work around them. If we were conscious enough to identify our own baggage and what triggers us, we could manage our reactions before they spill out onto our partner. Do you and your spouse take time to identify what triggers one another?

In extreme cases, it may be important to talk to a counselor or even a psychologist to see if things can be managed with personal growth tools or if medication might even be needed. When was the last time you unpacked your baggage in the light of day to see where criticism, dishonesty, or anger is holding your relationship back?

Go to our website (www.thegooddivorcebook.com) to take our relationship health survey. Assess where you fall on the spectrum.

YOUR GOOD DIVORCE CHECK LIST

A book is not complete without a handy checklist! So, here is ours. Doing all of these things will help you to create your own Good Divorce.

☐ Determine how you will divorce – (1) do-it-yourself, (2) mediator, (3) lawyer/court

☐ Research your rights if you've been married over 10 years.

☐ Design the outcome you and your spouse want for your divorce.

☐ Assemble your divorce team.

☐ Gather all financial documents in one place and share with your ex.

☐ Decide together how to make changes to your finances and insurance.

- ❏ Make an agreement to stop being in one another's business.

- ❏ Read books, attend seminars, and seek counseling to manage your emotional process.

- ❏ Move toward self-sufficiency by getting training, career coaching, etc.

- ❏ Design a parenting plan for being in the business of raising good kids.

- ❏ Wrap up loose ends in regards to various forms of paperwork.

- ❏ Move on to your brighter future once you have taken the steps to move through your transition with a focus on healing.

While these steps are meant to be all-inclusive, we may make adjustments to this checklist over time. Please check out our website for updates and additional tools to help you through your Good Divorce process.

www.thegooddivorcebook.com

ABOUT THE AUTHORS

ANDREW SILVERT, MBA, is currently a charter school executive and business consultant. He has had an eclectic career working as an Internet entrepreneur, math tutor, and massage therapist. Eight years of his adult life were spent in Tokyo, Japan where he became fluent in Japanese and developed a love for sushi and hot springs. His passion for this book comes from his own Good Divorce experience and his desire to share it with others. His story has had positive impact on friends and family, and he is excited to expand that influence to a much larger audience. Andy is the proud father of two sons who have both benefited from their Good Divorce experience. Pretty soon, he hopes to add "best-selling" author to his career resume.

BECKY SHOOK-WOTZKA, M.A., is a Psychology Practitioner who has been a Master Facilitator and Mediator supporting groups, couples, and individuals through conflict since 1996 (www.linkedin.com/in/beckyshook). Having worked with government, private companies, non-profits, and as an entrepreneur, she has seen conflict of all kinds at all depths. Her passion for this book comes from a desire for herself and for others to raise their consciousness in the skills needed to get along and resolve conflict. She is happily married, has two adoptive children (one from China and one from Vietnam), and manages a 4-generation, blended family household as the biggest conflict challenge she's had to facilitate to date.

———∽∾∾∽———

Guest Author, SONIKA TINKER, MSW, is a Relationship and Love Expert, Law of Attraction Coach, and Author of Seize Your Opportunities: Living a Life Without Limits. She and her husband, Christian Pedersen, are the founders of LoveWorks (www.loveworksforyou.com), a relationship training company offering leading-edge relationship solutions. They have over 40 years combined experience teaching singles and couples a radical new uplifting approach to life and relationship through numerous live trainings, online courses and coaching programs. Her contribution to this book, the crucial chapter on "dealing with an uncooperative spouse," gives readers powerful tools for dealing with challenging relationships in divorce.

Made in the USA
Charleston, SC
20 February 2014